T0326723

Troubled Hero

Troubled Hero

*A Medal of Honor, Vietnam,
and the War at Home*

Randy K. Mills

Indiana University Press

BLOOMINGTON AND INDIANAPOLIS

This book is a publication of

Indiana University Press
601 North Morton Street
Bloomington, IN 47404-3797 USA

http://iupress.indiana.edu

Telephone orders   800-842-6796
Fax orders   812-855-7931
Orders by e-mail   iuporder@indiana.edu

© 2006 by Randy K. Mills

Library of Congress Cataloging-in-Publication Data

Mills, Randy K.
  Troubled hero : a medal of honor, Vietnam, and the war at home / Randy K. Mills.
     p. cm.
  Includes bibliographical references and index.
  ISBN 0-253-34795-5 (cloth : alk. paper) 1. Kays, Kenneth M., (Kenneth Michael), 1949–1991 2. Medal of Honor—Biography. 3. Vietnamese Conflict, 1961–1975—Veterans—United States—Biography. 4. United States. Army—Medical personnel—Biography. 5. United States. Army. Airborne Division, 101st—Biography. 6. Post-traumatic stress disorder—Patients—United States—Biography. I. Title.
  U53.K39M556 2006
  959.704'37—dc22   2006006950

1 2 3 4 5 11 10 09 08 07 06

To those who endured that darkest of nights on Fire Support Base Maureen, 7 May 1970, and to those who died there: Robert Berger, Peter Cook, Lawrence Fletcher, Jose Gonzalez, Lloyd Jackson, Robert Lohenry, and Joseph Redmond.

And the officers shall speak further to the people, and they shall say, What man is there that is . . . tender-hearted? Let him go and return to his house, lest his brethren's heart [in war] faint as well as his heart.

Deuteronomy 20:8

Render therefore to all their dues: tribute to whom tribute is due; custom to whom custom; fear to whom fear; honor to whom honor.

Romans 13:7

Show me a hero and I'll show you a tragedy.

Anonymous

Contents

Acknowledgments

Many good people helped in the production of this book. I wish to thank Angie Carlen for her dedication in reading and typing through several drafts of the book, as well as her timely editorial suggestions. Thanks go also to Nora Nixon for her excellent transcribing of interviews. I am also grateful for help from the following people: Gib Rossetter, Steve "Greek" Avgerinos, Dick Doyle, John Smith, Mike Bookser, and Kurt Maag. They provided important information regarding the war in Vietnam after 1969, and they encouraged me to keep writing. Kurt's playful e-mails often got me through many a difficult day of research or writing.

Of essential help in gathering information and finding survivors of the 7 May 1970 battle at FSB Maureen was Alabama native Greg Phillips. Greg brought the same kind of determination in assisting me in the hard work of locating some of the fellows as he did that night so long ago at FSB Maureen when he rushed out from the safety of a foxhole to help defend 2nd Platoon's perimeter. Thanks, Greg!

Thanks also to the public library staff at Fairfield, Illinois, Kenneth Kays' hometown: Michelle Conard, Pam Woods, Mona Doty, and Kate Legge. They were most helpful in showing me where to find important material about Kays' early life. Randy Reed is responsible for first suggesting I write Kenny's story. Randy also connected me to several people who grew up with Kays. Other Fairfield folks who were of great help in writing the first part of the book were Joe Keoughan, Judith Puckett, Mike Pottorff, and Aaron Steiner. David Trovillion, a Fairfield native who now lives in New Jersey, offered important insight regarding Ken Kays' early Fairfield days as well. Kathy Tremper, a cousin of Ken Kays, also provided valuable information regarding the Kays family.

Thanks also to Indianapolis native Tony Cox, a 2nd Platoon man who also assisted me in connecting with other 2nd Platoon members and who shared a trip to Fairfield, Illinois, to visit Ken Kays' grave. Tony's early critique of a draft also helped greatly in getting the book on the right track. Another group that needs to be recognized for their help is the library staff at Oakland City University and especially Denise Pinnick and Stephanie Frederick. As always, your amazing patience is greatly appreciated.

Several people at Indiana University Press worked mightily to make this book come to life. I wish to thank Robert Sloan and Jane Quinet for their important contributions, especially in the editing process. Bob Sloan also made several important suggestions regarding content which greatly improved the flow of the book. Thanks go to Drew Bryan for his excellent copy editing work.

Finally, I wish to thank my wife, Roxanne Mills, who provided in-depth editing and other writing suggestions which made this book so much better.

Introduction

I'd Give My Immortal Soul for That Medal

In many ways the story of 101st Airborne medic Kenneth M. Kays captures a great portion of the paradoxes and ironies of our nation's long travail in Vietnam. Kays grew up in the conservative town of Fairfield, Illinois. As he moved into adolescence, the free-spirited Kays found his southern Illinois community especially restrictive, and his actions and his unique way of looking at things often provoked intolerance. One high school classmate remembered Kenny being ordered home by the principal to cut his long hair. The offbeat Kays returned to Fairfield High School with his head shaved. Fortunately, Kays would come to find solace in a small band of others like him. By his late high school years, the shy Kays could be found strumming his guitar and singing folk and protest songs, such as *Where Have All the Flowers Gone?* to a few close friends. Kays graduated from high school in 1967, just as the antiwar movement began to explode on the American scene. Kays' opinion about the war in Vietnam, while not completely formed, clearly leaned toward being against U.S. involvement there.

While attending Southern Illinois University, Kays' antiwar stance began to solidify. In the spring of his sophomore year, the young Fairfield native witnessed, amid great student unrest, the burning down of the university's landmark building, Old Main. Indeed, his time at the university saw vast turmoil and the emergence of a powerful counterculture which the Fairfield lad found himself drawn to. On the downside, the student unrest affected Kays' studies as well. By the spring term of 1969, the laid-back Kays was flunking out of school, but the happy-go-lucky youth did not seem bothered by this circumstance. Together with two of his friends from Wayne County, Illinois, the adventurous Kays journeyed to Woodstock in late summer of 1969. The three-day event in upstate New York attracted almost a half-million people and was destined to be the watershed episode for the American counterculture. The event seemed to be a turning point in the young man's life. By this time, the young Kays had determined he stood totally against the war, but because he had flunked out of Southern Illinois University, he received his draft notice two months after returning from his exhilarating pilgrimage to Woodstock. Not only did Kays stand utterly against the war, but few could have been more unsuited for the rigidness of the army than the long-haired young man from Fairfield, Illinois. Unable to get conscientious objector status, the southern Illinois man straightaway fled to Canada.

But Kays' unusual story does not stop there. Upon the pleas of his father John Kays, a local Fairfield businessman and World War II veteran, Kays reluctantly agreed to report to duty if he was allowed to be a medic. (He would refuse to carry a weapon once he arrived in Vietnam.) Perhaps both father and son believed the war was winding down anyway, as indeed it was, except for those luckless units, such as the 101st Airborne Division, that were located in a strategic area where the fighting still raged. Sent to the 101st, Kays would come to receive the Congressional Medal of Honor for his heroic, almost superhuman efforts on an isolated jungle mountain, Fire Support Base Maureen, on 7 May 1970. Assaulted by a vastly superior force of North Vietnamese regulars and elite sappers, Kays' isolated platoon fought desperately for survival. The ferociousness of the firefight at Maureen is evident in that the four highest awards for military valor, the Congressional Medal of Honor, the Distinguished Service Cross, the Silver Star, and the Bronze Star with "V" device, were given to four of the twenty-one men who endured this short but intensely bitter battle. More than a dozen Purple Hearts were also awarded. Almost half the platoon died in the melee.

The Congressional Medal of Honor is perhaps the United States' most prestigious recognition. President Truman once told a Korean War recipient, "I'd rather have this medal than be president." George S. Patton even offered to give his "immortal soul for that medal."[1] Of the hundreds of thousands of men who served during America's decade or so struggle in Vietnam, only 239 were honored with the medal, 70 percent of whom lost their lives for their actions. B. G. Burkett best summed up the rarity of the tribute in his book *Stolen Valor*. "For the impossible," Burkett noted, "one receives the Medal of Honor."[2]

In Kenneth Kays' case, however, the young man quickly came to vilify the medal. Given his unyielding antiwar stance, Kays refused to cut his long hair and beard for the medal presentation at the White House, causing the army to refuse to let Kays wear a uniform. Because of the young Fairfield man's wild, unkempt look, he was the last of nine men upon whom President Nixon pinned the medal. An extraordinarily private person, Kays seemed unable to make peace with that night at Fire Base Maureen or with the constant public scrutiny that came with receiving the most prestigious recognition our country offers. Kays further estranged himself from the town when he came back from the nation's capital and refused to allow the community to celebrate his accomplishment. He wanted no parade and soon sank into a sort of semi-seclusion.

Returning to his hometown of Fairfield, Illinois, after receiving the Medal of Honor, Kays often found himself in trouble with the law for his occasional bursts of weird behavior and for his heavy drug use. National news media promptly swooped down on Fairfield to examine these bizarre episodes, made more unusual by Ken Kays' Medal of Honor. Off-and-on visits to mental institutions followed as Kays slowly descended into a bleak depression, and over the next two decades Kays grew to become the town's local eccentric. Haunted by his demons, this tortured soul eventually took his own life in 1991.

Ken Kays' lonely sojourn can be better understood in the context of the stories of those who served in Vietnam after 1969, including those in the 101st Airborne Division. Their accounts have for the most part been neglected. Veterans of that era often hear others who served in Nam before 1969 say, "Oh yeah, you were there after the real fighting stopped." But for many of those who served after 1969, the war was even more atrocious, given that American soldiers had to now fight with the knowledge that the war was, for all practical purposes, over. Lewis Sorley, in his book A *Better War*, laments this glaring omission of studies which examine the last stage of the war. "Most better known treatments of the Vietnam War as a whole have given relatively little consideration to these later years. . . . To many people, therefore, the story of the early years seems to be the whole story of the war in Vietnam, a perception that is far from accurate."[3]

Caught in the perplexing shift to wind down America's part in the war were the tens of thousands of U.S. troops, such as Kenneth Kays, who were destined to fight in Vietnam after 1969. Gary Linderer, a 101st Airborne Ranger, captured the awful grimness of the circumstances for these particular men when he noted that by "the fall of 1969, the war, for all intents and purposes, had already peaked. 'Vietnamization' [turning the war over to the South Vietnamese] was the new buzz word, and Richard Nixon was keeping his promise by announcing troop withdrawals and a reduction in U.S. forces. To those of us who were there, the first indications of an army betrayed were just beginning to surface. No longer was there talk of defeating the enemy and achieving a just and final victory. Withdrawing with honor and grace became an acceptable alternative."[4] It would be left to the 101st to protect this difficult withdrawal. Perhaps the great cruelty of this portion of the war is best captured in the astute comment of one 101st platoon leader who wryly noted, "No one told us that the war was over."[5]

While Kenneth Kays struggled with the question of whether or not to stay in Canada in the late summer and early fall of 1969, several other young men, destined like Kays to serve in the 2nd Platoon, also wrestled with their individual fates. Since Kenneth Kays' voice has been stilled, their accounts are told here to add important context to Kays' story. Their stories also bring a wide spectrum of experiences concerning the war and, in that regard, add an even richer level of understanding to this unique part of the conflict.

As important as the war and its aftermath are to the story of Kenny Kays, so too is the region of Illinois where Kays grew to manhood. Settled primarily by upland southerners, this portion of the state, commonly referred to as "Little Egypt," carries a unique history which has long fascinated historians, sociologists, and the general public alike. Popular books about the area such as *Bloody Williamson, Murder in Little Egypt, The Other Illinois,* and *Brothers Notorious* bear testimony to this interest. Foremost in its colorful cultural history stands the area's emphasis upon individuality, along with a deep antiauthoritarian streak among many of its citizens. I believe that Kenny Kays' actions before, during, and after Vietnam were profoundly influenced by this culture. The political turmoil wrought by the ever-growing war in Vietnam and the great changes sweeping the country at the time of Kays' adolescence, especially the so-called counterculture movement which the young Fairfield man would come to embrace, may have also fed the antiauthoritarian spirit in Kays' world. Consequently, the political turmoil of the sixties will also be of interest.

Kenny Kays has found no peace in death and certainly little honor. At the time of this writing there is still little recognition in Kenny Kays' hometown of their native son's heroic actions in May of 1970. While other communities might indeed celebrate the kind of heroic deeds Kays performed, roads signs at the entrance to the city celebrate local teenage sports achievements–a third place in some state high school event, a second place in another–but do not mention Kenny Kays. Older residents, especially the World War II generation, often find it puzzling that some even wish to have Kays recognized. Mike Pottorff, a classmate of Kays', discovered the curious division when he was helping to place a small plaque honoring the Medal of Honor recipient at the courthouse square. More than one older citizen stopped and mentioned being disturbed by what the classmates were doing. Kays was a heavy drug user who lived a counterculture lifestyle, and his habits would certainly have been difficult for many in his community to understand or bear. On the other hand, a total lack of recognition seems equally out of place. There have been several letters recently sent to the *Wayne County Press* calling for this long overdue acknowledgment of Kays' service. In one piece, under the title, "National hero buried here and most are unaware of it," the writer complained, "if you asked the average person in Fairfield about this hero, their reaction would be a blank, unknowing stare."[6] All these letters carry one common theme: Kenneth Kays' bravery on 7 May 1970 needs to be recognized by the Fairfield community.

Although Kenneth Kays' story is briefly touched upon in Keith Nolan's *Ripcord* and Edward Murphy's *Vietnam Medal of Honor Heroes*, neither work presents the kind of depth and context that might bring understanding to Kays' experiences and the experiences of those draftees who endured combat after 1969. Further, my research suggests some inaccuracies in those accounts. It is hoped with a detailed telling of Kenneth Kays' story, along with the stories of several of his 101st comrades, appropriate honor might be given Kays and the other gallant men who fought the best they could in some of the most difficult circumstances in American military history.

Based on in-depth interviews, army unit histories and other official documents, local newspaper and national media accounts, personal letters, and Kenneth Kays' own personal writing journal, this book seeks to set the record straight. Ironically, from what I've come to know about Kenny, he probably would not have wanted this book written. That just seems to be in keeping with the reticence of this quiet and very private man. Still, I believe the world needs to hear Kenny's incredible story, for it concerns a part of that complex time when our nation found itself sending hundreds of thousands of her best young men to endure a war from which we would abruptly disengage. Perhaps if Ken Kays' restless ghost still walks the streets of Fairfield at night, it will find some peace in this story's telling.

Troubled Hero

Part I

I am a part of this people.

Abraham Lincoln, in an 1858 political speech given
in the section of Illinois known as "Little Egypt"

Southern Illinois is an intemperate land. . . .
Assaulted by great winds, great floods, and at
times by great and bitter passions.

Baker Brownell in *The Other Illinois*

1

Down in Egypt

If there existed a definitive moment of birth for Kenny Kays' generation, perhaps it was the election of John F. Kennedy in 1960. At the age of forty-two, Kennedy was the youngest man ever elected president and the first American president born in the twentieth century. Kennedy's inaugural address, delivered on a cloudless and cold January day in 1961, captivated the nation's imagination and captured the hope and expectations of the decade. Further, his vigor and youth stood in sharp contrast with the previous Eisenhower style. The new president's inaugural address conveyed both a powerful optimism and a profound challenge. "Let the word go forth from this time and place, to friend and foe alike, that the torch has been passed to a new generation of Americans." Foreshadowing our deeper involvement in Vietnam, the young president declared, "To those people in the huts and villages of half the globe struggling to break the bonds of mass misery, we pledge our best efforts to help them help themselves, for whatever period is required—not because the Communists may be doing it, not because we seek their votes, but because it is right. If a free society cannot help the many who are poor, it cannot save the few who are rich." Calling for "a struggle against the common enemies of man: tyranny, poverty, disease, and war," Kennedy promised "a new frontier" of opportunity and challenge. With the young president in office, a new aura of hope and excitement filled the air.

Unfortunately for the idealistic president, he inherited a deteriorated situation in Vietnam. Between 1950 and 1961, the U.S. had provided more than a billion dollars in aid and more than 1,500 economic and military advisors. These efforts supported the hope that the South Vietnamese government would grow to become a successful military force capable of standing on its own. By late 1961 however, President Diem, in a letter to Kennedy, called for more aid to help him in his effort to stop Communist growth in his country. "The Vietnamese nation now faces what is perhaps the gravest crisis in its long history," the desperate leader wrote. "If we lose this war, our people will be swallowed by the Communist Bloc."[1] At that time the cost to the U.S. of losing Vietnam far outweighed the cost of maintaining stability, and Kennedy, as did Eisenhower before him and Johnson afterwards, believed the U.S. would easily prevail against the more primitive Viet Cong and their brethren in the North if push came to shove. Consequently, the American president quickly responded positively to Diem's request. "We are prepared to help the Republic of Vietnam to protect its people and to preserve its independence," Kennedy replied. "We will promptly increase our assistance to your defense efforts."[2]

Most historians believe that had Kennedy lived he would have reached the same conclusion as Lyndon Johnson did in 1965 and committed the United States to war in Vietnam. That Kennedy was willing to defend America's continued involvement in Vietnam is made clear by his response to a letter from the sister of an American GI killed in Vietnam in January of 1963. In her letter to the president, Bobbie A. Pendergrass despaired, "If a war is worth fighting—isn't it worth fighting to win? Please answer this and help me and my family to reconcile ourselves to our loss and to feel that even though Jim died in Viet Nam—and it isn't our war—it wasn't in vain." "If Viet Nam should fall," replied Kennedy, "it will indicate to the people of Southeast Asia that complete Communist domination of their part of the world is almost inevitable. Your brother was in Viet Nam because the threat to the Vietnamese people is, in the long run, a threat to the Free World community, and ultimately a threat to us also." For that, the president wrote the grieving sister, her brother "did not die in vain."[3]

By late 1963, Diem's grip on the country continued to slip. A military coup, supported by Kennedy, carried out a takeover of the South Vietnamese government. In the process, and to Kennedy's horror, Diem was murdered. By this time Kennedy had increased the number of American advisors in Vietnam to more than 16,000 and had continued to send aid. Shortly after Diem's death, the president ordered an extensive review of how the United States "got into this country, what we thought we were doing there, and what we think we can do."[4] The American president would not live to see the report.

No one could have known it then, but with Kennedy's death came the death of hope for the younger generation that good and necessary change could be accomplished by working through the established system. Perhaps the clearest sign of this occurred less than a year after Kennedy's assassination in the form of the Free Speech Movement. In September of 1964, the chancellor of the University of California at Berkeley declared an area on campus used for organizing antidiscrimination meetings could no longer "be used for the mounting of social and political actions."[5] The chancellor's declaration led to mass protests, with the rallying cry being the right to free speech. Melvin Small pointed out the importance of this movement for later campus unrest in universities such as Southern Illinois University, the school Ken Kays would attend. The Free Speech Movement, noted Small, "captured the spirit of the times on many large campuses where students felt their individuality and freedoms were suppressed by institutions devoted to turning out white-collar professionals to maintain American capitalism." In addition, many of these institutions continued "rigid curriculum requirements, maintained curfews for women students, and enforced dress codes," further angering students.[6] For youths such as Kays, such restrictions would increasingly fan the flames of protest.

While international and national forces slowly conspired throughout the 1950s and early 1960s to bring the country ever deeper into the dark pit that would become the Vietnam War, and while the counterculture revolution loomed just on the horizon, folks in rural Wayne County, Illinois, and in the county seat of Fairfield, went about their daily lives in relative ignorance of events outside the region. On the surface, the community where Ken Kays grew up looked to be the perfect example of nostalgic Norman Rockwell America. Yet the rural community and the county stood as one of the most self-contradictory places in the country. Taylor Pensoneau, in his study of the gang violence which racked southern Illinois from the 1920s through the early 1950s, described Ken Kays' hometown as "a quintessence of small town America. An embodiment of a way of life fundamental to the early character of the country, far afield from urban sprawl. A place where traditional trappings were not sacrificed, even through the stagnant cycles of the region's up and down oil industry and other economic upheavals."[7]

In Kays' youth, outsiders often commented about the charm and friendliness of the community. The year Kenny Kays began as a sophomore at Fairfield High, city leaders placed large signs at the edges of town proclaiming "Fairfield. The city with a smile for you." Another set of earlier signs had declared Fairfield "The city of beautiful women." The community's conventional ways, which Ken Kays would eventually come to battle, can be understood to some degree by examining the local newspaper, *The Wayne County Press*, during the decade of the 1960s. Farming concerns most often headed the list of topics. A typical article noted, "The soybean crop in the Wayne City area is about 60 percent harvested now and yields are reasonably good."[8] Another headline and article lamented the previous year's poor harvest. "Wayne County farmers ended 1968 with less income from their crops due to lower prices and reduced yields!"[9] A feature column, "Soil and Water Conservation News," also touched on farming issues deemed important to this rural area. One piece noted how the then new technique of chisel plowing gave "farmers excellent erosion control the past two seasons in the Wayne County Soil and Water Conservation District."[10] Entire sections of the *Press* were devoted to relating the many happenings of annual farming celebrations such as "Bean Days" in nearby Wayne City. The tiny village, just west of Fairfield, contained fewer than a thousand souls yet would see ten times that number show up daily for the free food, carnival rides, and prizes the festival offered. Results of the *"Wayne County Press* Cooking School" also frequently took up an entire page.

Wayne County, because of its strong fundamentalist culture, had been the location of two earlier religious movements which had persuaded many people to leave their homes and jobs and band together to await the end of the world. Abundant stories in the *Press* during Ken Kays' adolescence announcing upcoming church "revivals" and church rallies also testify to the power of the conservative religious culture in the area. One article, for example, related the initial plans for an extensive religious "rally" which would hopefully become an evangelistic crusade of the caliber of a Billy Graham conference. Letters to the editor also demonstrate the penetrating religious conservatism of the area. One writer called for local media to tell more "about Christ and his coming and what was going to happen to people if they don't change their ways."[11] Another reader "urged more Bible reading. I believe without God this country will not stand long."[12]

These strong religious sentiments, typical of the region, did not bode well for anyone who had an inquiring mind or disliked authority. Indeed, there were those whose personalities just did not seem to fit the local norm. One young lady, for example, wrote to the *Press* during Kays' youth complaining of the critical opinions of many townspeople toward those who varied from traditional notions. "I would like to say that the sign at the edge of this town should be changed. It is not 'the town of friendly people,' or 'the city with a smile for you.'"[13]

Psychologically pummeled by the growing national turmoil that erupted in the mid-sixties, many residents grew increasingly more conservative as the decade progressed. The developing conservative reaction of the community to national changes can be seen in the writing of the *Press*'s primary columnist, Jack Vertrees, who, in one particular editorial in the late sixties, railed against one specific "liberal" antipoverty program. "We're gonna join the anti-poverty program and get us a $16,000 house. With no money down and only 1 percent interest on the easy payments. Its possible, or so said an FHA wheel at a Wabash Area anti-poverty meeting at Carmi some few days ago."[14] The drastic changes occurring with young people also caught the concern of Vertrees. In another column, the journalist eagerly related an article found in a St. Louis paper calling for the printing of the names of juvenile delinquents in local newspapers as a way of confronting expanding crime among youth. Concerned citizen letters often made it to the front pages of the *Press* in the middle and late sixties as well. Most vented conventional concerns, clamoring against the militant direction black protesters seemed to be taking or attacking welfare programs which seemed wasteful to local people who had been taught in the southern Illinois world of rugged individualism to make it on their own. Typical of these conservative readers, and there were many in the county, was one who wrote to the editor complaining of government waste. "The poverty game is a real big fake," this writer angrily declared.[15] Vertrees himself came to fear the growing disrespect for the law "deepening in America and of great concern."[16]

By the summer and fall of Ken Kays' sophomore year in high school, 1964, Republican leadership in the community had grown concerned over the choice of conservative Barry Goldwater as the Republican presidential candidate. The concern did not stem from Goldwater's rock-solid conservative views, but from his slim chances of defeating Lyndon Johnson. When the election dust settled, Goldwater had been mauled in a Johnson landslide. The *Wayne County Press* dutifully reported, "Democrats sweep nation in Tuesday's election." The state ticket was also glumly reported to have gone "all to Democrats." In Wayne County, however, Republicans easily won the majority of county contests, and as the press noted that "only one democratic state candidate carried Wayne County."[17]

Perhaps the greatest "liberal" challenge to Fairfield's seemingly picture-perfect conservative world in the 1960s involved a bitter contest between those who wanted to bring back the right to sell alcohol in Fairfield and those who vehemently sought to keep the county dry. The struggle demonstrates the odd dichotomy that Ken Kays would eventually face, a community split personality of sorts between a strong religious worldview and a more hidden desire for living on the edge of the law. Letters to the *Press* on the issue in 1969 clearly illustrate the commanding puritanical mood of the community, with most opponents of alcohol sales advancing a religious argument. Pastor James Clark explained, for example, "I am pastor of the General Baptist Church here, and as such, I will do everything that I am big enough to do to keep Fairfield dry. I believe Fairfield is as clean and good a town as I know of anywhere, why not keep it this way."[18] Another minister noted, "I have personally always been proud of Fairfield for its cleaned-up, neat, trim appearance. It has always had a unique, wholesome 'personality' of its own. But if liquor becomes available on a 'wet' basis, one had better get a picture now, the often-mentioned 'before' picture, for the 'after' picture will not only be not pretty, but it shall not even be worth taking."[19]

Not every reader, however, agreed with these arguments. One woman wrote to the *Press* pointing out what she considered to be the hypocrisy of such viewpoints. Her comments also indicate a darker side to the community and the region. "We have had prohibition in Wayne County for several years now. First question—Has it worked? No, it has not. This is the wettest dry county on the face of the earth. This county is not dry! Can you accept that people? The county is not dry! Anyone who wants a drink can get one through local clubs, from bootleggers, or can buy it in neighboring towns and bring it in. Among the first bits of information that any new-comer to town is given is the location of several bootleggers should he desire to patronize them."[20]

The seemingly idyllic world Wayne County offered to the outsider, an environment perpetuating a kind of Eisenhower-era world of black-and-white certainty, belied another more hidden element which flourished in the county and in that region of southern Illinois. In fact, the county and region had a long history that sheds some light on what was beneath the veneer of uprightness and conformity.

The region where Ken Kays grew to manhood had long been labeled "Egypt." Over time, the title was expanded to become "Little Egypt." Today tiny Wayne City proudly proclaims itself to be the "Bean Capital of Little Egypt," while Mt. Vernon, Illinois, the larger county seat of next-door neighbor Jefferson County, claims to be the "King City of Little Egypt," and so on. It remains unclear how the southern third of the state garnered this title. Perhaps the most logical explanation involved the region's reputation as the state's main source of corn, a basic food element to early pioneers, in 1830–31, "the winter of the deep snow." Since the only corn raised in the entire state that harsh, unusually cold year grew in the southern section, many settlers from the north rushed south for this basic food source. In the process, Illinois folks from both parts of the state were so reminded of the scripture in the book of Genesis that related "the famine was over all the face of the earth . . . and countries came into Egypt to buy grain. . . ." that the region became known as Egypt from that time on.[21] While this explanation carries a benign and gentle ring to it, the historic culture of "Egypt" has often been anything but gentle.

Historians and sociologists have long been fascinated with the unique upland South culture of the southern Illinois region. Richard Powell, in his authoritative study of the Midwest titled *Planting Corn Belt Culture*, pointed out that the triumph of New England/Yankee culture in the Midwest did not reach the bottom tier of the old Northwest. As for southern Illinois, "more than any other area of the North, this became the outpost of southern folkways which Yankees could never quite understand or modify."[22] People in this section were typically labeled by outsiders as poor, ignorant, lazy, and, oddly, arrogant, regarding their backwardness. Abraham Lincoln often made fun of people from the southern part of Illinois, usually starting such jokes with the phrase, "There was this man from Egypt. . . ." But Lincoln was himself a product of the Kentucky, southern Indiana, and Illinois frontiers, and during one of his debates with Stephen

A. Douglas in southern Illinois in 1858, he declared himself a part of this simple culture. "I am a part of this people," Lincoln proudly explained to the crowd at Anna-Jonesboro.[23]

Lincoln's pride in this culture aside, visitors to the area most often found the people and their harsh ways deeply disturbing. John Mason Peck, a Baptist missionary from the East, grew especially horrified at the backwardness of frontier southern Illinois people he came to work with. Writing of the people he first encountered in 1818, he observed that "a kind of half-savage life appeared to be their choice."[24] In the early 1800s, Morris Birkbeck, an Englishman, traveled to the immediate area of Ken Kays' birthplace where he, like so many other visitors, found himself staggered by the profound primitiveness of the people. Birkbeck also noted how the people of the region were not ashamed of their lifestyle, but rather stood fiercely proud of their ability to survive and also of their independence. "These hunters are as preserving as savages, and as indolent. They cultivate indolence as a privilege:-'You English are very industrious, but we have freedom.'" In another important assessment, the Englishman observed, "The simple maxim, that a man has a right to do any thing but injure his neighbor, is very broadly adopted into the practical as well as political code of this country."[25]

Birkbeck's observations regarding the region's love of individual liberty strongly suggests that freedom, especially the right to live and do as one pleased without restraint as long as it did not injure one's neighbor, stood as a primary birthright to these people. And while outsiders might ridicule this and other values of the upland southerners who settled the area, locals looked upon their way of life with great pride. These values—freedom to live one's life as one sees fit, pride, stubbornness, and a powerful streak of antiauthoritarianism—still echoed in the region by Ken Kays' time. Indeed, the antiauthoritarian streak so prominent in the region often evolved into a kind of secret worship of the outlaw type.

As time passed, the fierce independent attitude of the citizens of the region, along with occasional episodes of lawlessness, hardly diminished. In the 1950s, Paul Angle, an academic most famous for his Lincoln scholarship, grew so fascinated by the unique independent attitudes and violence often present in southern Illinois that he spent some time trying to develop an understanding of the phenomenon. He noted that most of southern Illinois "was settled by immigrants from Kentucky, Tennessee, the Carolinas, and Virginia. Many of them come from the hill regions, and they were slow to lose the peculiar characteristics of mountain folk. They were generous, hospitable, hardy, independent, brave, and intelligent, but undisciplined by education. . . . Almost without exception they were hot-blooded, proud, obstinate, jealous of family honor, and quick to resent an insult." Angle went on to examine the Klan and mining wars of the 1920s, followed by the bloody struggles between the Berger gang out of East St. Louis, Illinois, and Wayne County's own Shelton gang. Angle was especially taken by "the religious bigotry and nativistic narrowness" that plagued the region. "With the exception of Harlan County, Kentucky," wrote Angle, "I know of no other American location possessed of these attributes."[26]

Baker Brownell, a renowned social philosopher at Northwestern University, also took time to explore the uniqueness of southern Illinois culture. In his 1958 book *The Other Illinois*, he too noted the same stubbornness among the locals that Birkbeck had described so long before. Brownell thought the people of the region "silent, with a tough, arrogant silence. Their reticence is like the clay-pan soil of the plateau, stubborn, recalcitrant, unresponsive."[27] There also existed an odd bravado with the southern Illinois antihero. Gangster Charlie Berger, for example, proclaimed from the public gallows just before his own hanging at Benton, Illinois, "It's a beautiful world." Brownell dedicated an entire chapter, "A Catalogue of Villains," to the desperado types historically found in the area, including Wayne County's own Shelton brothers. One of the last "villains" discussed by Brownell shared an odd kinship with Ken Kays.

Arlie Pate, a Carbondale, Illinois, native, also served in an unpopular war. When the Korean War ended in 1953, Pate was one of two dozen or so captured American men who chose to stay in China, an act that stunned the nation. Brownell came to understand Pate's deeds as connected to the powerful local culture from which he came. "Greatness and villainy often have similar origins. The unregimented and willful southern Illinois country . . . has its social misfortunes and conflicts. It has its Arlie Pate, one of the twenty-three American prisoners in Korea who chose Red China, for a year or so at least, in preference to his home near Carbondale."[28] Like Ken Kays, Arlie Pate possessed an odd kind of nobleness, an air of stubborn defiance against all odds often seen in southern Illinois natives. Indeed, many southern Illinois residents found themselves enamored by Pate's adventures, perhaps seeing Arlie as a modern-day desperado folks from "Little Egypt" were so keen on. One Wayne County man, writing to the Carbondale newspaper on Pate's return in 1956, declared Pate's going to China as a "daring act of American youthful recklessness, the same that prompted the American youth 75 years ago to go west into a wild county infested with savage Indians, robbers, gamblers and cut throats and to eventually carve states and lay crude foundations for civilization."[29] The letter suggests the strength of the idealization of the outlaw in southern Illinois.

Brownell's own theory regarding Pate's actions was that "southern Illinois also has to a remarkable degree its individuals, its willful, flaming souls that consume life carelessly and with great heat. This fierceness of living that suddenly awakens in the stubborn folk of southern Illinois comes from men mutely looking for something. No doubt Arlie Pate was looking for something, or some place across inarticulate emptiness, across bitterness and uncertainty, a tragic sense of life where life and death converge—akin perhaps to the introverted death wish of which psychologists speak."[30] The Northwestern professor could just as easily have been speaking of Ken Kays.

When Kenneth Kays arrived into the world in the early autumn of 1948, the domination of the county and the region by the Shelton gang, unchecked up to that point, seemed to be coming to a violent conclusion. In 1950, *The Saturday Evening Post* had labeled the Sheltons "America's Bloodiest Gang."[31] After "Big" Carl Shelton was murdered on a lonely Wayne County back road in 1947, his funeral at Fairfield's First Method-ist Church was one of the largest in the town's history. Twelve hundred people crammed into the small church while more than eight hundred stood outside to pay their respects to the gunned-down gang leader. Taylor Pensoneau, in his book *Brothers Notorious: The Sheltons, Southern Illinois' Legendary Gangsters*, highlights the ongoing cultural staying power of the gangs' desperado story and strongly suggests its lingering influence over succeeding generations.

> Notorious. That was the word used more than any other to describe them. They became household names. Carl, Bernie and Big Earl, that is. Some people still quivered at the mention of their names decades after they were gone. They were, after all, central figures in a dark saga that ran beyond a quarter of a century, a captivating tale of murder, mayhem and sordid drama enveloping Illinois from its humblest nooks to the pinnacle of power. Few of the lives caught up in it all, and they were many, emerged unchanged. Like the James boys in the previous century, the Sheltons turned into the stuff of legends and lore. If some who knew them were to be believed, the Sheltons even displayed a Robin Hood touch here and there. Their reputation got so big that Hollywood once took an abbrevi-ated interest in their deeds.[32]

America has long harbored a hidden admiration for certain outlaw types, for example the long fascination with the likes of Jesse James, Billy the Kid, and Bonnie and Clyde, to name a few. Such admiration of the desperado element lingers even more in southern Illinois with the prior existence of groups such as the Shelton gang. Even today, stories of the ad-ventures of the Shelton boys abound. It is an odd point of status for a local to be able to claim possession of one of the hundreds of firearms the gang supposedly stored away for gang fights. For Kenny Kays, the gang culture which coexisted beside the moral conservative norm of Wayne County touched his own thinking. The area was simply haunted by the leftovers of the Sheltons' reign. Rod Cross, a childhood friend, remembered he and Kays talking throughout the years about the exploits of the Sheltons and other desperado types in the area as they drove by the places where illegal gambling, bootlegging, and gangland dynamiting and shootings had occurred.

Even by the mid-1960s, Wayne County still found itself connected with a gangster reputation in the form of Charlie "Blackie" Harris, a former member of the Shelton gang who turned on his ex-buddies and is believed to have murdered Carl Shelton in 1947. (Carl's murder was never solved.) Harris was responsible for more than thirty-two murders according to FBI files, and at the age of sixty-nine, he made the FBI's "Ten Most Wanted List." This would have been during Ken Kays' college and Woodstock days. By the end of the 1960s, Blackie Harris was serving a life sentence for the murders of two Wayne County citizens.

The ambivalent nature of the world Ken Kays was born to should not be underestimated. On one level there existed a powerful idealistic and conservative realm, typical of small-town America with its trim streets, family-owned shops, and abundant churches. As one local pointed out in a letter to the *Wayne County Press* as recently as 2002, "Fairfield has at least 15 churches in the city limits and probably 50 in Wayne County. We are a God loving, God fearing, Bible thumping community."[33] Even today, town leaders describe the community as a city of trees and picture-perfect side streets. These bright and traditional aspects would have been profoundly difficult to live with for someone who valued the freedom to be different and who also carried the hidden antiauthority mentality which was so powerfully woven into "Little Egypt's" cultural fabric.

But even outlaws such as the Sheltons still had to respond in many instances to certain unstated rules of social decorum. They often cooperated enough with the common folks around them to be thought of as living an alternative but not an undesirable lifestyle. They could occasionally convey the touch of a Robin Hood or a good-time Charlie. Thus it was possible to live successfully in this conservative area and still live on the fringe, or even beyond, if one was "gallant" in a roguish sort of way. As we shall see, tragically, Kays never seemed to be able to compromise in this regard. His desire for individual freedom ruled his beliefs and actions. On the frontier, such a worldview might have not only been tolerated, but also exalted. In a more modern situation, such a value system could lead one into great trouble.

2

Where Have All the Flowers Gone?

The big news in Wayne County in the late forties revolved around two events. The first concerned the slipping grip of the Shelton gang on the community. The brothers had made many enemies through the years and would now reap a bitter and deadly harvest. On 24 May 1949, Big Earl Shelton was seriously wounded by one of three shots fired through a window of the gangs' gambling center, the Farmers' Club, located on the Fairfield courthouse square. Successful assassinations of several of the gang members would soon follow. Three years after the attack on Big Earl, a powerful blast that "broke windows all around the square,"[1] rocked the Farmers' Club, knocking it out of business.

The second event which raised much interest in the community involved the ongoing exploration for oil. One *Wayne County Press* edition recounted, "Perry Fulk is believed to have a good well in Jasper Township about five miles northeast of town." The paper went on to report that the well was in "wildcat territory," meaning that drillers there were not connected with any major oil well companies. Given the independent mindset of the people of the area, it is not surprising to find that wildcatters were frequent in the Wayne County portion of the southern Illinois oilfields. Two weeks later the *Press* declared that the Jasper oil pool was "a hot spot in Wayne County."[2] Despite the wealth that the oil boom would produce, Fairfield at that time still lacked a hospital. Most residents who needed hospitalization traveled the fifteen or so miles west to the much larger city of Mt. Vernon, which boasted two hospitals. There, in the self-styled "King City of Little Egypt," Kenneth Michael Kays entered the world on 22 September 1948.

Parents John and Ethel Kays were known to be a bit eccentric, but were also considered good, productive citizens. Kenny would be their only child. John Kays, like so many others of his generation in Fairfield, had fought in World War II, the so-called good war, and, typical of most of those folks living in the Eisenhower 1950s, completely trusted the government to carry out its job of maintaining a peaceful status quo environment so that hard-working citizens could enjoy the fruits of their labor. In stature a small man—he was short and weighed less than 150 pounds—Johnny Kays stood tough and wiry as well. Born in Wayne County in 1913, the elder Kays graduated from Fairfield High School in 1932. A hard-working entrepreneur, Kays once operated the B&K Airport, worked at Fairfield's Airtex Products, and later ran his own grocery. Like many veterans of World War II, Kays was also active in the town's Masonic Lodge. A feisty competitor, the elder Kays at one time played semipro baseball for the local Fairfield "Hoppers" in his younger days. Rodney Cross, a childhood friend of Ken Kays, remembered how his own father, Marion Cross, and John Kays played together on the community's semipro team. "The two men were best friends and shared the same birthday. Even by my day, John Kays was very much his own man and a rather stubborn individual," Cross recalled.

The "Hoppers" team, for which Kays and Cross played, performed competitively enough to be asked to play an exhibition game against the St. Louis Cardinals. A team photo taken about this time shows a young John Kays, kneeling next to his best friend Marion Cross, looking back into the camera with an expression of a somber confidence. Jon Simpson, a later neighbor of Kays', remembered how "Johnny Kays brought in the first airport here. He had an awful lot of get up and go." Aaron Steiner remembered John Kays as small but spunky. "Ethel Kays I recall more vividly. She was a real tell-it-like-it-is person." Ethel Kays, born in 1907, came to Illinois from nearby Indiana. She served several years as the secretary for the local Chamber of Commerce and sold insurance for the Royal Neighbor Insurance Company. As these observations suggest, John and Ethel Kays seemed to accept their community's values and the limitations which these norms fostered. Their only son Kenny, however, seemed to have inherited his parents' intensity, but not their cooperative worldview.

One of Ken Kays' best friends, Joe Keoughan, has many strong memories of his unusual companion, especially of Kays' insistence on being his own kind of person. "Kenny Kays and I grew up together. We attended grade school, high school, and college together. Kenny was unique—I understood that from the beginning. Most of all, he was a high-energy person with a great sense of humor. On the other hand, he could be sort of shy when he wasn't with his friends." One particular image of Kenny stands out in Keoughan's mind even today. "I remember a teenage Kenny running down this railroad track—just took off for no apparent reason—while smoking this big fat cigar. He looked like a damn train." Smoking cigars turned out to be one of Kays' most common indulgences during his adolescent years. "Kenny really enjoyed his cigars. He'd mail order them special and then smoke them in front of the high school—a rather bold thing to do in

Better days: Kenny Kays played four years for the Fairfield High School Mules football team. Kays is number 29, front row of this 1964 freshman team photo. Courtesy Randy Reed.

that day." Kays also took great pleasure in keeping in shape, perhaps as a way of building up self-esteem. "He enjoyed running and martial arts," his best friend recalled, "as well as weight lifting." Many of Kays' acquaintances also remembered the young man's amazing upper-body strength.

David Steiner, like Joe Keoughan, was also a close friend to Kays. "We both were on the football team; we spent many times together hiking, camping, rock climbing, and other youthful sports." Steiner mostly remembered Kays as "a sensitive, artistic, humorous intellectual. He played the tuba in the school band and the guitar, accompanying his own singing. He was also an avid reader, particularly science fiction." Kenny and David devoted lots of time to "the game of chess, and he and I would take turns trying to best one another." They also shared an unusual sense of humor that was not fully recognized or appreciated by others in a small-town atmosphere.

Another sign of Kays' creative life came in the form of photography. David Steiner remembered how his friend "set up a darkroom in his house and practiced photography. He and I made our own senior yearbook photos, along with Mike Feldman. As a result our portrait photos possessed a quality unlike any of our classmates' taken by a local photographer. The yearbook committee accepted Kenny's and Mike's picture, but rejected mine, and as a result I do not appear in my senior class yearbook." The Steiner-Kays friendship can be seen in a photo of the two teenage boys taken in 1967. Kenny has a baby blue jay perched on either shoulder, while David stands close behind his friend. Both wear beguiling, innocent smiles.

Aaron Steiner, a younger brother of David's, frequently observed Kays' awesome strength as well as his toughness. "He'd be jumping on a trampoline at school, doing flips and stuff and occasionally he'd bounce off and hit the ground in a hard and awkward position. But he'd just jump right back up and go back on the tramp." Many years later, after heavy drug use had taken its toll, Kays still possessed amazing strength. Rod Cross, another boyhood friend, discovered this reality the hard way one evening. "Kenny was still a block of muscle even as he aged. If he got mad, he made a fight quick. One night I was at his place, and I had been drinking and giving him a hard time. Kenny just picked me up and threw me out of the house. As I got up, I said to myself, 'Well, I guess Kenny had enough of that.'"

Kays entered Fairfield High School in the fall of 1963, just three months before President Kennedy's death in Dallas. Like other schools in Midwest America at that time, Fairfield High had yet to see the explosion of drug use or the existence of a youth counterculture. An odd fad called "piano wrecking" was the popular antiauthority pastime on college campuses in those innocent days, and the Beatles had yet to make their appearance on American soil. Teenage boys, especially athletes, wore crew cuts or flattops. "Driving the circuit" stood as the ultimate pastime for Fairfield youth on both weeknights and weekends. David Steiner recalled, "There are two major one-way streets that run the length of Fairfield. Together they form a loop of infinite circulation that can be modulated by trips by friends' houses along connecting side streets and extended to epicycle through the city park. Taken in its entirety, it is called 'the circuit.'" Driving around Fairfield also meant teenagers "pausing for momentary meetings in the parking lots and drive-ins, making connections, finding out where the party will be tonight." Once the party places became known, cars would "fly out of town and down the gravel roads of rural Wayne County to the designated spot for the night, generally to some farmhouse, a barn, or just an open field."

In 1963–64, Kays' freshman photos appeared in the high school yearbook. One picture showed a smiling, bashful-looking adolescent sitting on the front row with the Fairfield freshman football team. A year later Kays' face could be found with other members of the Latin Club and school band. Kays, too short and uncoordinated for baseball or basketball, did fairly well in football, where his unusual upper-body strength served him well. Sometimes, however, Kenny had to endure some not-so-kind teasing. Kenny Boster recalled the freshman football coach giving Kays the nickname "the missing link" because of his unique build and head shape. "This thoughtless label hurt Kenny deeply." Another fellow football player remembered Kays being called "Kenny crude" because of his unusual size and shape. Yet another label heaped on Kays was "Neanderthal." When friend David Steiner asked Kays how he felt about that nickname, "Kenny just smiled and said, 'I prefer Cro-Magnon.'" Rod Cross remembered the uncommon kind of athletic ability his friend Kenny Kays possessed. "He was so strong in his arms, chest, and shoulders. He'd do parallel bars stuff at the halftime of basketball games. But this was at a school where basketball was king and that kind of skill was just not appreciated."

Cross's observation that Kays' unique athletic skills were not respected stood as particularly true, given the region's almost irrational love of one particular sport. In Fairfield, as in the rest of that region of southern Illinois, basketball reigned. The local Fairfield paper frequently carried long and gushing articles concerning successful "Mule" basketball teams. One article enthusiastically declared of one notable sixties team, for example, "There's never been anybody like them! That's the 13-and-0 Fairfield Mules, with the longest basketball win streak ever for a Fairfield High team. They're a mixture of city boys and country boys, one tall boy and several short ones, but they jell together like peas in a pod and give a bread and butter performance with every game."[3] Kenny played on the less-popular football team all four years in high school, and in his senior year the football Mules won three games while losing seven. Still, as Rod Cross noted, Ken Kays clearly resided on the fringe at best when it came to sports popularity at Fairfield High.

Many remember Kays as a cutup and a prankster. Close friends recall that Kays could grow quiet and shy around other students or around authority. It did not help matters that Kays' sometimes atypical behavior often ran against the norm in a town which annually held a Tom Sawyer and Becky Thatcher look-alike day at the city park. And while he played football, joined the Latin Club for a year, and played in the high school band, his shyness and lack of interest in academic success or pleasing either his teachers or his peers often left him something of an outcast.

On rare occasions, Kays could be extraordinarily gutsy, especially in a situation where he sensed his individual rights were threatened. Terry McGaha recalled a time when the high school principal ordered Kays home to get his long hair cut, crew cuts and flattops being the general order of the day. Kays left but returned with his head completely shaved! Then there was the time when Kays and David Steiner slipped into Fairfield High School and stacked "the study hall desks into a colossal six-desk-high pyramid in honor of educational monotony." Rural communities have typically tolerated youth "sowing their wild oats," especially in southern Illinois, where independence-driven conduct stands as something of a quasi-norm. But Kays' and his friends' behavior likely began to raise the concern of Fairfield citizens for reasons outside of the local culture.

By Kays' sophomore year in high school, 1964, town leaders had grown concerned with the disturbing changes in teenage behavior across the nation. One concerned mother wrote to the *Press* that she would like to see stricter rules on the way teenagers dressed at Fairfield High School. Referring to a recent article about the rules set down by the principal of another nearby high school, the woman remarked, "I wish this were done here . . . sure would be a help to us old fashioned mothers." The rules she wished were enforced at Fairfield High would ban "pegged trousers and jeans for

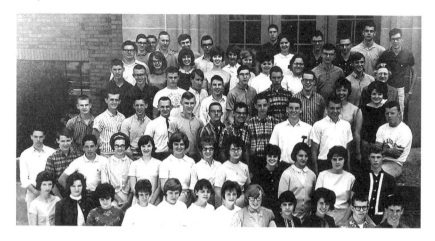

Kenny Kays, though not always a good student, was highly intelligent. Photo of his junior year Latin class. Kays is on the bottom row, second from right. Courtesy Randy Reed.

the boys," while T-shirts would "not . . . be worn as an outside shirt and all shirts must have at least a quarter length sleeve." Girls would not permitted to "wear slacks or shorts to school or school functions." Loose-fitting slacks could be worn to football games. Stretch pants would be banned. Girls' skirts would come "at least halfway down the knee. Elaborate hairdos are also on the forbidden list."[4]

In response to the "concerned" woman's letter, another parent, who seemed more aware of Wayne County's lawless past, wrote, "To me we don't have a problem with our teenagers nearly as much as we do with the adults of our town. We need to give our teenagers more credit instead of always disagreeing with what they do or what they have done. . . . I say we adults of Wayne County should take inventory and ask ourselves: Do we live up to our standards? . . . I say we have a fine group of teenagers. Anyway they are willing to take their punishment for the crime they've committed. Just how many of our adult crimes are solved in Wayne County? When I look around and see how immature a large majority of our adults appear, it disgusts me to no end. Then to think they'll sit back and complain about these 'modern teenagers.' Let's not forget we were all teenagers at one time, and we certainly were not perfect."[5] This less judgmental position regarding youth in Wayne County, however, seemed to be a minority opinion. *Press* columnist Jack Vertrees, for example, complained about how "things are going to go to pot if the guys are going to look like girls."[6] It was at this same time that Ken Kays was ordered home by the high school principal to cut his long hair.

In the spring of Kays' senior year, a local judge ordered a teenage offender to shave off his beard and keep it shaved for six months as a part of his sentence, a drastic step Judge Quindry had employed before. Earlier a young man had been ordered by the judge to "clean up and get his 'duck-tail' hair style trimmed." Quindry explained to the *Press* how "some teenagers use long hair or beards as a symbol of rebellion. Often they seem not to know what they are rebelling against though."[7] The judge's order to shave off the beard touched off an intense debate. A few vocal young people wrote to the *Press* complaining about the older generation's attitude. One angry youth argued, "If an older man can wear a beard, why not a young man—and if a boy wants their hair long whose business is it but theirs?" *Wayne County Press*'s Jack Vertrees, however, responded, "Maybe nobody will admit it anymore, but we still think it holds true, sloppiness begets sloppiness, and there's a difference between a neat beard and a bird's nest."[8] Other fiery letters on the subject soon came to rest on the newspaper editor's desk. A former resident, now a teacher at Columbia University in New York City, hurriedly penned the *Press* complaining, "I can see no logic in the Judge's reasoning. On the surface it seems ridiculous. Are we to assume bearded men are 'bad' and making them shave will make them 'good'? Or is shaving some kind of punishment?"[9] Most older Wayne County citizens, however, strongly supported the judge's decision.

As these kinds of debates between and among generations began to increase, small numbers of young people in the Fairfield community were beginning to come together to form groups. Music, especially some of the newer, more controversial, songs, contained mantras for these groups, while drugs, mostly pot, often stood at the heart of their social communion. Changes in the kind of music youth listened to in the sixties stood as yet another disturbing element with which older Americans, including older Fairfield citizens, struggled. Many songs now seemed to celebrate casual sex and drug use and often contained antiauthority themes. Todd Gitlin, in his book, *The Sixties: Years of Hope, Days of Rage*, argues that the 1965 antiwar, antiauthority song "Eve of Destruction" stood as a turning point in counterculture music. "In August 1965, within five weeks after its release, 'Eve of Destruction' surged to the top of the sales charts. . . . This was a song which a vociferous group of campus barnstormers called the Christian Anti-Communist Crusade said was 'obviously aimed at instilling fear in our teenagers as well as a sense of hopelessness,' helping induce the American public to surrender to atheistic international Communism. . . . Pop music devotees react to the mood of a song whether or not they grasp the lyrics. . . . Plainly," assessed Gitlin, "a new constellation of moods was in the air. 'Eve of Destruction' seemed to certify that a mass movement of the American young was upon us."[10] By the middle and late sixties, songs such

Kenneth M. Kays, Fairfield, Illinois, High School senior year photo, 1967. Courtesy Randy Reed.

as "Come Together," originally released by Jefferson Airplane and later by the Youngbloods, called for a new level of peace and harmony among diverse groups. As Vietnam grew more intense, antiwar songs increased. Buffalo Springfield belted out "For What It's Worth" while Creedence Clearwater Revival lamented the injustice of the war in their 1967 release "Fortunate Son." These tunes and others underscored the turbulent times which surrounded Ken Kays and no doubt influenced his beliefs about his world and his place in it.

By the mid sixties, town leaders and concerned citizens began to take actions to prevent improper music from influencing the young people of the Fairfield area. One constructive way the older generation found was the construction of a youth center called the Kon-Tiki. The music there was bouncy and innocent as were the Sadie Hawkins dances where girls were given a chance to ask out their own dates and dress up as hillbilly couples. Benign groups such as the Koinsmen and the Corvettes, both from Evansville, Indiana, often supplied the beat after the big game. *Press* columnist Jack Vertrees strongly commended the initial endeavor by noting, "A word of praise to a group of kids who have proved the last three or four weeks that 'enterprise' is still a word in their dictionary. We're talking about the FCHS Kon-Tiki builders who have transformed the community center into a Tahitian masterpiece."[11] The *Wayne County Press* also carried a column called "With Love, Cathy" penned by Fairfield High School student Cathy Love. Reports about the goings-on at the Kon-Tiki often stood at the heart of her commentaries. The column captured much of the innocence of that time, but tellingly, Ken Kays' name, as well as the names of Kays' friends, rarely made it into Cathy Love's articles.

Terry McGaha, a year older than Kays, remembered the Kon-Tiki center as a place "for the good kids. If you were not in the popular crowd, or from the wrong side of the tracks, you probably didn't go there." Kays, however, was an occasional exception to this rule. "Kenny had the type of personality that he could fit in if it was important to him." Best friend Joe Keoughan recalled how Kays "liked folk music and playing his guitar." Sometimes Kenny would get up enough courage to play and sing at the Kon-Tiki. "He especially liked to sing antiwar songs like 'Where Have All the Flowers Gone?' This was in 1967, the height of the Vietnam War. Kenny was always antiwar, although his intensity about Vietnam grew much greater once he got to college." Kays' fondness for this particular protest song suggests important clues regarding the quiet young man's personal feelings about the great changes occurring around him, especially the growing conflict in Vietnam. The last three stanzas in particular speaks of the senselessness of war.

Despite Kays' unbending insistence on authenticity and his inability to blend in with the in-crowd, the young teenager managed to find a core collection of friends who, like Kenny, saw themselves as outside the domain of jocks, cheerleaders, and the Kon-Tiki crowd. Together, Kenny Kays, Dave Steiner and his brothers Aaron and Brad, Joe Keoughan, Rodney Cross, a.k.a. R-O-D, and a few others, created a tight and supportive community of their own. Many in this group were highly creative and had a budding interest in the arts, and one problem for them and others like them was the lack of offerings for young people in Fairfield who wished to participate in art venues rather than sports, driving the circuit, or just hanging out at the 'Tiki.' The *Press* offered a glimpse of this problem in one particular 1964 article. Noting how a "determined group of thespians," had attempted to bring two one-act plays to the community, the article went on to forecast that the endeavor was likely doomed to failure. As Jack Vertrees summed it up, "The group realized that live theater is not everyone's dish in a town such as Fairfield."[12] Nevertheless, Kays' band of outsiders still discovered unusual ways to remedy this lack of local support for the arts.

The Steiner brothers especially loved to make home movies in which Kays' group of friends would dress up and perform stories cooked up by David Steiner. The group met and socialized at the city's French Park at a shelter house which sat close to the Steiner family's home. Joe Keoughan remembered one movie the group made "where a duck was caught and supposedly roasted and then put on a platter. However, when the top was pulled off the plate, a talking human head appeared in place of the cooked duck." The outgoing and confident Dave Steiner would often talk the group into dressing up for the whimsical, slapped-together plays he had written. These pieces were frequently recorded, and somewhere a film may still exist of the days when the sometimes shy Kenny Kays performed before the camera with some of his friends.

During the latter part of their high school years and over college summer breaks, the "park gang" began putting on regular theatrical pieces. "We'd post handbills along the circuit," David Steiner recalled. "Sometimes we'd have an open mike, and Rodney Cross and I would try to convince the local storytellers to come in and tell their tales. Many of the stories were quite good." Once Kays himself was the headliner for one of the week's shows. "He was on to play his guitar and sing, but thirty minutes before the show he had not shown up, so we rushed over to his house. All the lights were out and no one seemed to be there. We just kept banging on the door and finally here comes Kenny. He was in one of his moods, didn't want to play, but we made him anyway."

David Steiner enjoyed pushing the limits of social decorum in the small conservative town. Middle brother Aaron remembered how David relished "making things happen. He'd try to get a group of young people to pull off some kind of event just to see if he could motivate it to occur. Having access to a variety of clothing, Dave often dressed himself and sometimes his friends in offbeat ways." In 1967, when Joe Keoughan and Ken Kays trekked down to Carbondale, Illinois, to attend Southern Illinois University, David went north to the University of Illinois. In the summer, however, they would all come back to Fairfield. It was during one such summer that Steiner carried off a particularly memorable event. "David had organized a group of young people to perform skits at the little amphitheater in the park," Aaron Steiner recalled. "Dave named the group 'Real Eyes.' It was mostly the crowd that had run together in high school. Anyway, one summer David got the support of the town park board to do a play he had written called *Nothing Ever Happens Here*. A big crowd of folks, many of them Fairfield elite, came to the opening of the theatrical performance. "David kept them waiting in the summer heat for quite a while, then he came out in a tuxedo with a spotlight on him. By that time the audience had grown especially restless. When Dave walked out on the stage everyone grew quiet. He thanked them for coming and related that he hoped they would soon return. Then he shrugged his shoulders as if to say 'nothing ever happens here' and walked off the stage." While Fairfield attendees may have felt taken by the unusual performance, David Steiner sincerely considered the event as cutting-edge art.

Many years later, after fleeing to New York City, David Steiner wrote a short, sarcastic piece in an attempt to capture what he perceived as the town's narrowness. The essay, titled "Fairfield," captures the kind of bitterness which could occur when teenagers such as Steiner and Ken Kays failed to fit into the conservative norm. The piece read in part, "Fairfield was a nice little town, once. The county was settled by a bunch of cowboys of one type or another. Yet among all 6006 residents, there was not one Indian. Neither were there any Negroes, nor any Chinamen. In fact, there were no people who even claimed to be Democrats. Every one was pretty much alike. Except for one thing, it was hard to tell any difference at all. Some claimed they were Methodists and others claimed they were Baptists. The Methodists said you shouldn't drink, but they did anyway; the Baptists said you shouldn't drink and they didn't. Maybe it was the other way around, but it was sure hard to tell which was worse."

As far out as David Steiner could be, his off-the-wall antics and overall views about life in general, and Fairfield in particular, came as a lifesaver for Ken Kays. Joe Keoughan recalled, "In high school Kenny hung around me and David Steiner mostly. Dave was a straight-A student, tremendously intelligent and a sort of alter-ego for Kenny." While Kenny could be shy and shunned the limelight, David Steiner thrived on pushing people's buttons—a daring thing to do in a conservative town such as Fairfield. Keoughan recalled, "Sometimes Dave would dress up completely in black—and I mean completely—or conversely in total white and come to school that way. One Sunday morning Steiner, dressed in gym shorts, went to several churches in town and bounced a basketball to the front of each congregation in the high school basketball–crazed town. Then he would hand the startled minister a note which read 'Jesus Christ is a whole 'nother ball game.' Of course no one had a clue what this meant." The David Steiner basketball escapade eventually grew to a legend. No two people today tell the story quite the same way. Younger brother Aaron Steiner recalled, for example, that David "went into about six different churches on Sunday morning dressed in red shorts and white high top socks. He dribbled up to the front and handed each minister a card with a drawing of a cross and a basketball goal on it and the words "what is your goal for Christ?'"

Some years later, while in college for the second time and after returning from Vietnam, Kenny wrote a poem about David and himself spending a day relaxing on a college campus. The lighthearted piece, entitled *Lunch Hour*, gives some insight into Kays' and Steiner's important relationship.

> Dave is in the sun
> I am in the shade
> We're resting in the air
> Where many a squirrel has played.

He rests in the sun
I delight in the shade
The dove is in the air
And the bunny in the glade.

He's still in the sun
I'm here in the shade
What a party we could have
If somebody'd bring some ade.

In every stanza of the poem, David is always seen as staying in the sunlight, while Kenny lingers perpetually in the shade. It is of some interest that Kenny Kays perceived himself as always in the shade, the half-light of things. As time passed, however, this half-light seemed to grow darker. Much of this swelling darkness came from Kays' interest in drugs.

Rod Cross remembers the beginning of the drug culture in Wayne County and Kenny Kays' participation. "It was something you kept under your hat more than today. There was Steiner, Kays, me, and two or three others were all that were in the pot scene at first. The park was one important location where drug activity first began to happen in the community. Interested youth could go to the park to make a connection about where a party would take place and where drugs would be available. In the beginning there were only two or three dozen kids involved." But tiny Fairfield wasn't the only place where rising drug use among the young existed in the sixties. The problem had grown to epidemic proportions on a national scale.

In 1967, Kays' senior year in high school, *Newsweek* magazine took an in-depth look at the exploding use of drugs by youth in a special 1967 piece titled *Trouble in Hippieland*.[13] Much was made in the magazine of the connection between music and drug use. The editor of *Teen* magazine claimed, "We have . . . indicted psychedelic radio as a prime force in spreading the hippie philosophy."[14] In a later issue that year, *Newsweek* noted, "The use of drugs—from chalky white diet pills that give Dexedrine highs to red, yellow, and blue LSD capsules—has spread throughout the youth population. Drug use," the article warned, "is no longer concentrated among the liberal campuses of the East and West coast or the megaversities of the Mid-west."[15] Counterculture critics and conservatives also grew alarmed about the growing lack of moral centeredness which appeared to be sweeping the nation. Another special report in *Newsweek* lamented, "The old taboos are dead or dying. A new, more permissive society is taking shape. Its outlines are etched most prominently in the arts—in the increasing nudity and frankness of today's films, in the blunt, often obscene language seemingly endemic in American novels and plays, in the candid lyrics of pop songs and the undress of the avant-garde ballet, in erotic art and television talk shows, in freer fashion and franker advertising."[16]

Local Fairfield concerns over possible counterculture activities and increased drug use among Fairfield teenagers multiplied when police stumbled upon paraphernalia for glue sniffing at the county fairgrounds just west of the city in the spring of Ken Kays' senior year. A front-page article in the local paper announced, "The glue sniffers are here! But one sniff too much and they might be gone—to a not so happy hunting grounds. That's the fear of Fairfield police officers after evidence was uncovered here Wednesday that some people have been engaged in the dangerous practice of glue sniffing to get their kicks. It's a cheap form of getting on a drunk or LSD jag and just as dangerous."[17]

While local community leaders struggled with concerns over music and drug use by local youth, as well as the new rebellious fashions some wore, another darker force hovered just on the horizon. The war in Vietnam, however remote to Kays during his high school years, would have lingered ominously at the fringe of any young American male's consciousness as that young man moved closer to draft age. In one fashion or another, the war was always there, even in rural towns such as Fairfield. In late 1964, the *Wayne County Press* noted the first local soldier wounded in Vietnam. "A former Wayne County boy, Robert R. Hutchcraft, is lying in a Viet Nam hospital after being critically wounded in action Sunday night in the 'undeclared war' there. He was shot in the arm and stomach and is believed to be the first casualty of this action from Wayne County."[18] In another front-page article that same year, the *Press* quoted returning Fairfield soldier Bill Hoffee, who told local folks, "Our army, navy, marines, and air force are all doing their jobs well in Vietnam. The cooperation between the forces is outstanding. . . . We're there and we're winning. It's a lengthy process, however. It will probably be years before we can come to terms. The Viet Cong and the North Vietnamese are learning that we plan to stay there until our objectives are obtained."[19]

By the late sixties the war had grown to become a nightly feature of American television. The news was most often discouraging. For example, on 27 February 1968, Walter Cronkite of CBS television told millions of Americans, "To say that we are closer to victory today is to believe, in the face of evidence, the optimists who have been wrong in the past. It seems now more certain than ever that the bloody experience of Vietnam is to end in a stalemate." Other national media conveyed the same depressing news. In April 1967, *Newsweek* recounted "the bloodiest week" in the war. More disturbing perhaps to someone of draft age such as Ken Kays loomed the constant reports in national news media which described the specific kinds of injuries American fighting men suffered. The local Fairfield paper could be just as graphic in its account of wounded local men. Among other things, reports told of different Wayne County men missing in action, being paralyzed from the neck down, and having limbs amputated. A few Wayne County natives had given up their lives by the time Kays approached draft age. Such local reports, and the gossip they likely created, would have made it impossible for young Wayne County men such as Ken Kays to entirely ignore the war.

It was not only the fighting in Vietnam that bedeviled the nation and Fairfield, Illinois, in the late sixties. In the spring of 1967, television screens and newspapers were filled with accounts of student-led demonstrations erupting all across the country. In small towns such as Fairfield, these events were a constant subject of wonder and scorn. *Newsweek* described the largest national demonstrations of the war to that date as having "draft-card burnings, Viet Cong flags, 'peace' balloons and flag draped coffin floats, and their banners identified the diverse collection of marchers as Quakers, Roman Catholic, Jewish war veterans, Episcopal seminarians and students from at least a score of universities. Mostly they were young, but there was also a liberal sprinkling of middle-class marchers in business suits and housewives with children in baby buggies. They were out to protest the war in Vietnam, in the largest demonstration to date."[20]

Conversely, support for the war among most Fairfield citizens could be seen by a large Flag Day parade planned for that same spring. The *Press* observed that the event would be a clear effort "to show the boys in Vietnam the people of Fairfield are behind them. . . . It will show our fighting men that we aren't all draft card burners back home."[21] For some young draft-age men such as Kays, all this media bantering may have meant the war had become a happening not worth dying for. Kenny Kays also had another, more personal, reason for being disturbed by the war. A portrait of an older, never-seen half-brother, killed in a previous war, sat on top of the Kays' family television in a blond wood frame. Kenny would have seen the photo every day of his life, a grim reminder, since childhood, of the cost of war.

Fortunately, by the fall of 1967, Kays had obtained a college exemption from the draft and consequently would not have to deal with the problem as long as he remained in school. The lucky young man could now look forward to heading off for Southern Illinois University in Carbondale, a school well-known for being a hard-core party school. Friend Joe Keoughan believes Kenny Kays had always been against the war, though during his high school years Kays' position perhaps lacked understanding and empowerment. Southern Illinois University, and later Woodstock, were destined to change all that. Meanwhile, Kays faced one more event involving authority before he escaped Fairfield High School forever.

High school baccalaureates and graduations in the sixties in southern Illinois communities were typically uncomfortable affairs with seniors wearing hot gowns in non–air-conditioned gymnasiums. At the stifling 1967 Sunday baccalaureate for Fairfield graduates, minister Dale Warren urged the young audience "to live lives designed by God. Go forth in Christian ideals. The world is hungering for this kind of leadership."[22] We do not know if young Kays was moved by the minister's conservative sentiments. David Steiner (today David goes by his mother's maiden name of Trovillion), however, recently noted that while Kenny Kays' 1967 yearbook photo carries the caption "every inch of his height is an inch of mischief," had he been allowed to choose his own motto, it would have been "Give it hell, it'll be alright."

3

A Party School

The college experience often occurs as a defining event in the lives of American youth. This was perhaps even more so in the middle and late sixties for rural and small-town kids who came to large, state-supported universities. Kenny Kays' sojourn at Southern Illinois University certainly had much to do with his own later decisions and actions regarding the war in Vietnam. Looking at this aspect of Kays' life also brings sharper focus to our nation's struggle at home regarding our involvement in southeast Asia. But to understand Kays' experiences at Carbondale from 1967 to 1969, one must also examine the legend of Delyte Morris, who, like the Shelton boys and Arlie Pate, represented yet another southern Illinois original. Morris came by his southern Illinois ways naturally. His parents began their married life in a one-room log cabin with a lean-to just outside the tiny village of Xenia, a few miles northwest of Ken Kays' community of Fairfield. Southern Illinois folklore insisted that a child named after a deceased person would die young, so when an earlier son named after a deceased relative died in an accident, the superstitions Lillie Morris made up completely one-of-a-kind names, Lossie and Delyte, for her next two children. There on a hardscrabble southern Illinois farm, the two Morris boys labored daily to feed livestock and milk fifteen cows.[1]

Delyte Morris's hard upbringing eventually paid off. Though it was the middle of the Great Depression, the tough and determined young man, with strong support from his parents, earned a Ph.D. from the University of Iowa. By 1945, Morris had been considered for the presidency of Southern Illinois University, but he failed to get the approval because Chester Lay had better qualifications. Fate, however, intervened. In August of 1948, as Delyte Morris labored to build an outdoor privy at a summer cottage in Maine, he received word from Carbondale, Illinois, that President Lay had resigned. Morris accepted an invitation to take the vacated position, and he would later preside over the longest and largest expansion in the university's history. Unfortunately, like Ken Kays, Morris was destined to become something of a tragic figure. For a brief time fate would throw the two southern Illinois natives together.

The new university president clearly understood the uniqueness of "Little Egypt" and the need of the region to have a large state school. In his 1949 inaugural address, Morris noted, "In our location at the southern end of a northern state with a geography, climate, a population, a folklore, an economy, and an agriculture more South than North, there is need for the development of a program to fit the regional characteristics of the area to be served."[2] Words, however, could not conceal the daunting task the novice administrator faced. The southern part of the state had long been neglected by the political power brokers at Springfield and Chicago, especially regarding education. Morris was more than up to the task.

Baker Brownell, who himself was lured away from Northwestern University in the 1950s to take a faculty position at SIU, once dubbed the Carbondale school "Delyte's new suitcase college." In the late fifties, Brownell noted the sudden explosive expansion of the school. "For more than eighty years the roots of Southern Illinois University have been quietly searching the stubborn soil. Now, suddenly, this state university has begun an unexampled growth. This huge educational bulge down state helps to confirm the claim that sad, burned-over, impoverished land between the rivers has vast American potentialities." Brownell laid the reasons for the once-struggling school's success directly at Delyte Morris's feet. "This suitcase college," declared Brownell, was without a doubt Morris's doing and was "clearly the liveliest thing in southern Illinois."[3] Many now called the once-struggling institution Little Egypt's Cinderella school.

Applying what one biographer called "warm paternalism," Morris soon became immensely popular on campus. One observer of college life in Carbondale in the 1950s remembered Morris and his wife, Dorothy, frequently walking or riding bicycles around campus in the evenings. At such times Morris stopped students and talked with them, "often not identifying himself but simply striking a conversation along some line of their reflection on their being on campus. Also, especially in these years, he frequented the halls of classroom buildings. It was not at all unusual, if one were working in a departmental office in Old Main, for instance, to look up and see him going down the hall, taking in all that he saw. He took a personal interest in everything."[4] By the mid-sixties, Carbondale was anything but a "suitcase college." In 1964, *Time* magazine carried an article on SIU and Morris entitled "Big Voice in Little Egypt," which highlighted Morris's down-to-earth commitment to taking "the University to the people."[5] The summer of Ken Kays' freshman year at SIU, *Newsweek* also recognized Delyte Morris's astounding accomplishments. "Delyte Morris, with the instincts of a born promoter, has pushed SIU into the mainstream of academic affluence," the highly complimentary piece noted.[6]

A year later the *Christian Science Monitor* declared, "They said it couldn't be done. But Southern Illinois University (SIU) has quietly defied the predictions. Though far from the city life, with well-worked mines and barren farmland on every side, it has somehow jumped the gap from a struggling teachers college to one of the nation's 20 largest universities." The article further noted that "most of the credit for the vigorous recruiting in staff . . . and students and the confidence that success was possible is given to Delyte W. Morris, now in his 20th year as the university's eighth president. And, as much as he might deny it, the faculty here insists that SIU is still very definitely a 'one man show.'"[7]

Unfortunately, Morris would not survive the changes the 1960s would bring. One university official explained his downfall by saying that Morris, in his early sixties by the time of student unrest, "reacted pretty much the same during the years, but the students changed. He had a high level of concern for student affairs and their conduct. He expected them to be ladies and gentlemen."[8] But by 1966, the counterculture did not react to watermelon festivals and simple platitudes the way earlier students had, and Morris's benevolent, often dictatorial style often angered them as well. Students at SIU, like so many other students of the time, sought empowerment and sometimes outright radical change. In October of 1970, the *Daily Egyptian* carried a story in which Morris summed up his frustrations with this new type of student. "I find myself flabbergasted by some things I hear students say and do today."[9]

For Ken Kays, Carbondale offered not only an escape from the draft but a whole new exciting world, so different from the conservative one he had known in Fairfield. Kenny arrived on the Southern Illinois University campus at Carbondale in 1967, just as college response to the war was heating up. Here Kays would meet more like him, outsiders to the system which prevailed in small-town America. Good friend Joe Keoughan, who also attended SIU then, turned Kenny on to the non-violent resistance ideas of Gandhi and the philosophies of Hinduism and Buddhism, and Kays began to establish his own collection of books on these subjects. "Kenny came to believe more and more in the idea of reincarnation," believed Keoughan. "He also began to read all the radical magazines and papers available at Carbondale. He had always been against the war, but his Carbondale experiences made him more so. He was a true conscientious objector and not just someone who was afraid he'd get killed in Nam."

In a larger context, antiwar historian Melvin Small noted that, in general, college students at this time "were agitated over many things, including paternalistic administrations and rigid curriculums. In the early sixties, many college administrations enforced dress codes and curfews for coeds, and some even sent students' grades to their parents. The key issues then on campus involved those related to *in loco parentis*; off campus it was civil rights. But by the late sixties, in part because many of the *in loco parentis* practices had been dropped, students were most concerned about the war and the draft and related issues of classified research and recruiting for the military and military industries on campus."[10] Conversely, Small observed that only 10 percent or so of U.S. universities and colleges "experienced violent disturbances during the war, and on those campuses, fewer than ten percent of students were activists." Yet these few demonstrations "were less important than the attention they received from the media and the general sympathy they enjoyed from many students and faculty members."[11]

The environment at Carbondale, especially the protests, could have only strengthened Kays' thinking regarding the war and society in general. Brian Clardy, in his book about Illinois state political leadership's responses to student unrest in the late sixties, believed SIU possessed several unique elements which led to especially volatile student protests there. The student rights' movement at Carbondale "tended to focus on free speech issues and the question of shared university governance between students and administrators." This movement also sought to change the university's policy on visitation hours in coed dormitories. The most notable emergence of this movement concerned "a massive student walk out of Neely Hall in April 1969 to protest the university's housing policy."[12] Another force for radical change at the southern Illinois school was the student New Left, which "sought to address many of the issues relating to free speech, ideological discourse on campus, and opposition to the war in Vietnam. Grounded in an autonomous chapter of SDS [the radical Students for a Democratic Society], and the creation of the Southern Illinois Peace Committee (SIPC), the student New Left movement used university facilities to get their message across. It attempted in many respects, to pull the students' right movement leftward."[13] As noted, SIU would develop a reputation as one of the most intense party schools in the country, along with a reputation as a school which thumbed its nose at authority. The school had witnessed a large-scale riot the year prior to Ken Kays' coming and students had gotten a good taste of the excitement such an event could create. Leaders of the university were shocked by the intensity of the uproar, and local law enforcement was overwhelmed by the sheer numbers of students involved. Any youth chafed by a small-town environment would certainly be refreshed and excited by the changes Carbondale offered.

Violence and protest at Carbondale and other campus unrest across the nation stirred much national concern. One national magazine also noted the growing social division caused by the war during Kays' freshman term at SIU. "So incendiary have feelings become that close-knit families have had to agree to disagree about Vietnam at the table. Ministers have become alienated from their flocks, parents from their children, teachers from their students and from each other, blacks from whites, hawks from doves. . . . More than anything, Vietnam has made Americans question their fundamental assumptions about themselves and their country."[14]

In the late fall of 1967, Ken Kays' parents, along with other parents who had sons and daughters attending school at Carbondale, received an unusual letter from President Morris. In part, the letter declared, "This is a period of unusual tension and stress in American life. This tension reflects itself to a peculiar degree on the campuses of our colleges and universities. I believe that the best service the University can render to its students and indeed to its country at the present time is to cling to its traditional position of objective analysis and free discussions."[15]

The growing unrest at SIU followed the typical national pattern. Throughout April of Kays' freshman year, university leaders struggled with the difficult question of student free speech and dissent. The *Daily Egyptian*, the university's student newspaper, carried an ample number of articles on these events. On 26 April 1967, the "Voice of the People" column of the *Daily Egyptian* included letters from Tim Webber on "Social Reform Overdue at SIU" and from Bernard Flynn, assistant professor of philosophy, calling for suspension of all classes at Carbondale until questions regarding free speech, the right to protest, and the war were addressed. Also, that same month, a three-hour resistance rally, a volatile meeting sponsored by the Southern Illinois Peace Committee, took place next to the Morris library. Toward the last of the month, seven hundred students marched in protest on campus, and by the first of May, a student newspaper story told of a plan by students to take over the University Center. At the top of the list of complaints stood military recruitment, with students demanding "an immediate and permanent end to military recruiting on campus." Clearly, Kays was exposed to a tremendous amount of antiwar fury during his freshman year.

When he returned to Carbondale for his sophomore year, student discord had greatly multiplied. Morris, in an interview with the *Christian Science Monitor*, related his own deep concerns at that time. "It's my feeling that universities are going to be destroyed if we're not very careful. This university is not insensitive to student feeling, but it will not be run by a minority . . . of 'sometime students.'"[16] Regardless of Morris's belief that the trouble he faced on campus came from a small group of "sometime students," by 1968–69, the southern Illinois native had clearly lost the respect and support of those attending the campus. Late in the 1969 spring semester, almost three thousand students carried out a major sit-in. The local Carbondale paper noted, "At several points a group of 15–20 militants demands immediate action. . . . About 25 police, wearing helmets and armed with night sticks, were stationed behind the Morris home."[17] The average southern Illinois resident became greatly disturbed by goings-on at Carbondale. Kays' neighbors back in Fairfield took a particularly dim view of what was occurring nationwide and at Carbondale around the time Kenny attended there. A front-page *Press* article, for example, told of a panel of local SIU students who rushed to Fairfield to discuss "student unrest on the campus" with local citizens in an attempt to ease concerns there.[18] Jack Vertrees expressed his own view regarding events in Carbondale by reporting the following story in the *Press*: "It was midnight Thursday and the phone rang in a Fairfield home. 'Mom,' the voice said, 'I want you to come and get me out of this town.'" The voice was a Fairfield girl in Carbondale on the SIU campus, scared at what was happening in that riot-torn campus town. Vertrees pointed out, "This didn't happen in New York or Baltimore, Chicago or Berkeley. Nope, in Carbondale, just 90 miles from Fairfield." Vertrees went on to observe that the story represented "a sign of the times we live in. Fear creeps in. Deeper and deeper. This wasn't the only such call made to parents here this past week. There were others, and the students came home, just like the one above. Crazy world . . . getting crazier."[19]

A young female student wrote Vertrees and attempted to explain what college students were trying to get across. Vertrees responded, "There is much wrong with America today. But is burning down the campuses the way to solve those problems?"[20] Stronger anti–higher education letters followed. One offended man asked "if there are others nauseated, frustrated and totally disgusted" at the things going on in Carbondale.[21] Petitions even circulated through the town to request state authority "to enforce all of our laws dealing with riots, mob action, and related state laws and university regulations." The petition further called for "those arrested to face the full charges for their offenses, including expulsion where the university regulations so provide."[22]

By this time several forces had united and now threatened to tear apart the very social fabric of the nation. The civil rights movement and the explosive growth of the counterculture, with its drug use, strange and bizarre dress, and way-out music, greatly troubled the average American. But it was the war in Vietnam that provided the core energy to the stormy sixties. As one historian noted, "Anti-war youth and hippies faded together like tie-dye." After the well-attended antiwar march on the Pentagon in 1967, participant Keith Lampe wrote, "Just two weeks ago we were talking about 'hippies' of 'the psychedelic movement' on the one hand, and 'straight peace activists' or 'resisters' as something quite distinct. Now the two are tightly communal aspects of the same thing—and who can hang a name on it?"[23]

Concerns about the counterculture influence among Wayne County folks during Kays' stay at SIU eventually took the form of an ongoing debate in the *Wayne County Press* over the hippie lifestyle, as well as the war. The narratives give further focus to the bitter feelings Kays, with his long hair and counterculture lifestyle, would face in his community when he was home from school and later from Vietnam. The controversy began when a Fairfield couple wrote an open letter to their son serving in Vietnam. In the letter, which appeared in the *Press,* the couple praised the conservative training their son had received and condemned "hippies, yippies, and draft card burners."[24] A Wayne County serviceman who stopped in California on his way to Vietnam added some heat to the debate when his letter appeared in the *Press.* "I would just as soon be in Vietnam as here," he wrote, "for I get tired of going into the towns around the base and seeing the long-haired peace lovers. The other day I was asked to sign a petition to send to their congressmen to stop the war. That is all there is around here—hippies! These people disgust me. . . . It's a 'weak, sick, and ignorant' generation. You wouldn't believe it until you come here. For my money they can lock them up and throw away the key!"[25]

A teenager Kays' own age, from nearby Johnsonville, took offense at the letter and offered this response: "I find I must use the old argument of 'What is so wrong with long hair and beards?' People seem to forget so easily. They judge people by appearance. Look around, people, find a picture of Jesus. How is he portrayed? Most of the pictures I have seen have shown him with long hair. Believe me Jesus was a peace lover."[26] Another young writer of like conviction wrote, "I am sick of hearing about this younger generation which does not care, of being labeled a coward, a Communist, or an atheist, and of being stereotyped as a 'hippy.' The majority of young Americans do care and want to remain proud of the American flag. All we ask is to be given a chance to prove our capabilities."[27] Most correspondence to the *Press,* however, agreed with the first soldier's critical assessment of youth. One firmly declared, "They say people have every right to protest and march in these so called peace marches; but in my opinion they do not have the right when it means risking the lives of our servicemen and harming our country."[28]

Joe Keoughan maintains that while Ken Kays read radical literature during his time at Carbondale, he never became directly involved in radical political movements against the war. Kays' agenda seemed to be more in keeping with his southern Illinois upbringing—if I'm not hurting you, then leave me alone to do my own thing. However, on a personal level,

Kays' Carbondale experiences had apparently shaped his view of the war and his own sense of how he would react if drafted.

During the summer of 1968, Kays came home from Carbondale to work construction for a local farmer named Robert "Pud" Williams, another southern Illinois personality. Selected by maverick Democratic governor Dan Walker to serve as the head of the state's agricultural department in the early 1970s, the colorful "down home" Williams was considered "good copy" for the press because of his country witticisms.

A conversation Williams overheard in 1968 underscores Kays' growing opposition to the war. Williams recalled, "I first knew Kenny Kays when he and many of his friends, fresh out of high school, helped my family build the concrete grain elevator at Golden Gate in 1968. I remember listening to the young men talk about the Vietnam War; some of the older ones had received their draft notices. And I recall hearing Kenny Kays say that he knew he wouldn't carry a gun and didn't know if he would accept his draft notice."[29] The politically connected Williams was greatly impressed by the youth's sincerity, but such straightforward consideration of this volatile and complex issue in so conservative an environment was typical of Kays. Later, Pud Williams would use his substantial influence to try to help the Kays family when Kenny began to struggle with the demons he brought home from Vietnam.

While the war hovered like a bad dream over the Carbondale landscape, there were other temptations for small-town kids like Kenny Kays. Southern Illinois University carried a reputation as a party school, and it offered Kenny his first chance to experiment with drugs beyond the small amounts of pot he and some of his friends had smoked back in Fairfield. During Kays' time at Carbondale, the president of SIU's student body had twice submitted a bill to legalize marijuana on the campus and had also asked the university's security police to adopt a "more liberal attitude" on the issue. David Steiner bluntly recalled Kenny's increased drug use. "When I went off to the University of Illinois, Kenny went to Southern Illinois University whose image was more relaxed. And, while we both seemed to major in the sixties, he proved the more dedicated and dropped out to devote serious attention to the connoisseurship of drugs." Despite the growing pains that often come with the college experience, one could still see much of the old Kenny there at SIU. "Kenny had little fear of consequence, of getting hurt—of death," recalled friend Joe Keoughan. "He was always trying something new. Once he jumped an Illinois Central freight train in Carbondale and rode it down to Fulton, Kentucky. He later told me how the train would hurtle through each crossing and town and he'd just give a big wave to anyone who'd happen to be watching."

Unfortunately Kenny's increased use of alcohol and drugs while at Carbondale, along with all the ongoing student unrest, eventually led to his failing in school. Marshall Mills, an SIU student who came from the same area of Ken Kays' community of Fairfield, recalled how difficult it was to maintain any level of academic work during that time. "SIU was just a party school anyway, but with the war going on, there were always protests and people shouting at each other. I had a psych class, for example, that was very interesting, but the professor didn't make anyone study. He just seemed very distracted with all that was going on. Many instructors were in sympathy with the students on the war and wanted the place closed down. Drugs were everywhere too. I remembered my roommate made his own LSD. It was just an incredibly hard environment in which to study. The whole world seemed to be going nuts there." During the most severe riot people were "running through the streets naked" and "smoking dope on the streets. It was a circus atmosphere," remembered one rioter, "a lot of fun."[30]

Perhaps the final blow for Kays' educational endeavors at SIU involved the burning down of "Old Main," the oldest building and the premier icon of the institution, in June of 1969. The *Daily Egyptian* reported how President Morris, "clad in a light green sport shirt, [was] ushered out of the burning building earlier in the morning as he was attempting to salvage some valuable manuscripts."[31] At the time of the fire, Old Main was home to the University museum, offices for all teaching assistants in the department of English, a foreign languages teaching laboratory, the Air Force ROTC rifle range, and fourteen classrooms. Many believed the burning of Old Main came as a result of antiwar sentiment toward Vietnam. At the time of the fire, SIU was home to an institute for Vietnam studies, for which it had received federal money, and some believed the Vietnam study center was a front for CIA operations. Burning Old Main down got rid of the ROTC facility and made a statement about the Vietnam center.

On the day of the fire, an aged and shaken Delyte Morris talked to a news reporter, telling him the fire was "terrible, just terrible."[32] By 1970, Morris had stepped down following controversy over his attempt to build an expensive president's house without going through the proper channels. A close friend of Morris later bemoaned, "If only he had quit five years ago, or even three. He would have been a saint on campus by now. It was terribly unfortunate he did not."[33]

Ken Kays' own abrupt departure from SIU made him eligible for the draft, but by this time Kays could take solace in the fact that the war seemed to be winding down. The draft board in Wayne County, for example, had already begun cutting back on the numbers they were requiring from the county, and national news media consistently reported that President Nixon seemed committed to bring more troops home. One report suggested the war would be settled by Christmas. Leaders in Nixon's own administration expressed confidence that North Vietnam would agree to a mutual troop withdrawal. At the same time, U.S. casualty rates lowered for a while, further conveying an illusion that the war might soon be over. Rod Cross believed Kays had resigned himself to take his chances, hoping he'd not be called. He also knew Kays would seek conscientious objector status if selected. Kays could take hope from a ruling in a Massachusetts court case in April of 1969, just before Kays had flunked out of school, in which the court ruled that a young man could qualify for the CO exemption for non-religious reasons. The always laid-back Kays waited to see how the draft problem would work itself out.

4

I Felt I Was Born That Weekend

The year 1968–69 was an extraordinarily difficult year on campuses all across the nation. Graduation ceremonies across the country during the late spring of 1969 continued to reflect the ongoing tensions and struggles found on campuses nationwide. Commencement speakers often found themselves heckled or challenged by the graduates, while peace signs adorned the tops of numerous mortarboards. Some graduating students simply stood up and walked out of their own commencement exercises. Students at Berkeley shook their fists at their parents who themselves were "booing the student speaker." *Newsweek* observed of these tense ceremonies, "The spirit of student protest, it seems, has infected commencement exercises, and whatever else might be said, graduation day wasn't dull." Perhaps the most disturbing and insightful graduation speech came from a student at Harvard who told the adult leaders there, "For attempting to achieve the values which you have taught us to cherish, your response has been astounding. It has escalated from the presence of police on the campuses to their use of clubs and gas." The disgruntled student went on to explain, "I have asked many of my classmates what they wanted me to say today. 'Talk with them about hypocrisy,' most of them said. 'Tell them they have broken the best heads in the country. . . . 'Tell them they have destroyed our confidence and lost our respect.'"[1] This student's thoughts captured much of the frustration of many college students that spring.

In May of 1969, Ken Kays left the unsettled campus at Carbondale after failing the spring term of his sophomore year. Although he was leaving the university, the time spent there, outside the conservative culture of his small hometown, had acutely shaped Kays' views and made the young man's return to Fairfield more difficult. Hunkered down back in Fairfield, he now found himself spending much more time paying close attention to the national news for signs of how the war in Vietnam fared. The news was mixed. During April, strong hints of a resolution of the war could be found in numerous news media accounts. The United States was in intense negotiations with North Vietnam, causing some top-level leaders to predict "a negotiated settlement in the war by December." It was also reported in April that American troops were being restricted to "ground combat operations that are absolutely necessary."[2] Then came May. National media that month carried detailed and disturbing information about an intense and bitter battle which took place on Ap Bia Mountain/Hill 937 or, as it became known, Hamburger Hill. The fight there only increased the soaring tensions at home while moving many young American men of draft age to wonder what they might do if faced with induction.

By any traditional standard of warfare, the fight for Hamburger Hill would have been measured as a success and become a rich source for future military war lore. But given the rapidly deteriorating attitudes at home, the breaking story of the savage battle had just the opposite effect. *Newsweek* reported, for example, "by military standards, the troops of the 101st Division had not only done their job. They had done it heroically. In the face of superior numbers and murderous fire, they had rammed the enemy off Hamburger Hill and inflicted losses possibly ten times as heavy as they had suffered." Conversely, the report noted, "It was a memorable military achievement, and yet the question could not be repressed: Was it worth it?"[3]

Newly chosen Senate majority whip Edward Kennedy leapt to attack military leaders and the administration, calling the battle "an outrage" on the Senate floor. He labeled the repeated attacks on a hill which he claimed possessed no military significance as "senseless and irresponsible." American soldiers, he declared, "are too valuable to be sacrificed for a false sense of military praise."[4] The Nixon administration quickly employed damage control and denied they were stepping up a war the president had promised to disengage from "with honor." A month after the ill-fated battle, the Pentagon reported in response to the ongoing criticism coming after Hamburger Hill, "our operations have not increased. In fact they are down about 8 percent below the level of a year ago."[5]

Young Kays might have been further moved to question having anything to do with the war if he had read a series of letters addressed to Senator Kennedy written by American soldiers who fought on Hamburger Hill, which eventually were published in *Harper's Magazine*. Reporter Neil Sheehan noted their disturbing power. "Now for the first time, some at least, of those simple soldiers who had once cheered 'all the way,' no longer believe. Through their letters . . . flows bitterness." One medic with the 101st Division wrote, "I want to thank you for standing up for us in Vietnam. Men like you are on our side. Perhaps if more of your colleagues join with you, I will make it home to my wife." Another 101st trooper lamented, "I don't suppose any war has ever been pleasant, nor has anyone suggested it to be.

So while watching my partner under the 'buddy system' get shot six times in both legs going up the hill, or seeing one guy in my foxhole get shot in the mouth, when we finally reached the top, I was simply more depressed than angered." The embittered soldier went on to add, "For if we are indeed going to fight a war, all the horrors are certainly going to be there too. No, the test must be whether the war, with all of its attendant insanity, is worth the price. . . . It is simply a fact that this war was a mistake."[6]

Perhaps pressured by such opinions, the Nixon administration, by late May and on into June, began to publicly tout a plan to withdraw from Vietnam. Further good news was that North Vietnam also seemed ready to negotiate an end to the war as well. On 8 June, Nixon announced the withdrawal of 25,000 American troops and the acceleration of a plan to turn over the fighting to the South Vietnamese. By August the president's popularity had popped up in the Gallup polls to 65 percent—the highest of his seven months in office. But then, in that same month, news media told the disturbing story of an entire company which refused to engage in combat. Kays could not have missed the detailed accounts of the episode. The Associated Press related, "Interviewed in the field, a group of the soldiers said the whole company was together in refusing to obey orders after five days of hard fighting because, as one of them put it, 'Morale was at rock bottom.' None of the soldiers who heard this contradicted the statement." Explained one army private, "The whole company definitely was behind the refusal. None of us thought we would withstand being pinned down another day or spend another night out there."[7]

As the summer of 1969 wore on, the rural community of Fairfield, despite the turmoil, still maintained much of its all-American quaintness and surface calm. Pretty and statuesque Nikki Lynn Riley won the Miss Wayne County Fair title that sun-drenched summer, and visitors still commented on the attractiveness of the town. Men with farmer's tans, along with their families, confidently strolled the Fairfield streets on Saturday mornings, coming in for haircuts and groceries. During the quiet summer evenings, along the many tree-lined streets, the ceaseless clamor of night insects filled the air. Meanwhile, in mid-August, Ken Kays first heard from his friend David Steiner of an event that would forever change his life.

Music was the core of the worldview of most young people in the late sixties. It reflected how they felt and believed as well as suggested what things they might want to change about themselves and the world around them. Ken Kays and his friends were no different, but unlike many of the youth in Fairfield, Illinois, Kays and his group preferred the offbeat stuff. Kays himself enjoyed folk music, which he liked to sing as he strummed a guitar. Kays' friend David Steiner had gotten into blues music while attending the University of Illinois, and in early August of 1969, the adventurous

Fairfield lad hitchhiked to Michigan to attend the first Ann Arbor Blues and Jazz Festival. There Steiner recalled hearing some "of the greatest blues artists ever." Steiner was so elated by the goings-on at Ann Arbor that he made plans then and there to get his group of friends back home to attend the next available national music event. News was soon circulating at the Ann Arbor concert of another music festival to be held in upstate New York, advertised as "The Woodstock Music and Art Fair, An Aquarian Exposition." Steiner, who loved more than anything else to make things happen, just knew he had "to go back to Fairfield and get a group of people to go."

Steiner's hope for bringing a large throng of Wayne County young people to Woodstock, however, soon faded. "As time went by, more and more people dropped out—I had thought we'd be able to get at least one car full." In the end only Rod Cross, David Steiner, and Kenny Kays loaded up in August of 1969 to make the historic trek to Woodstock. The three Wayne County youths made an unusual band—Steiner with his tall, lanky build; Kays, who was short and a solid block of muscle; and Rod Cross who, due to a childhood illness, stood barely five feet four inches tall and carried no fat at all on his slight body. The mischievous Cross went by the initials of his first name: R-O-D.

But even with the firm commitment made by the three friends to make the journey, the trip almost did not happen. Initially Steiner hoped that the group would find suitable transportation among the other youths going to Woodstock. But then, as more and more dropped out, so did the possibility of decent transportation. Rod Cross drove a beat-up metallic blue Chevelle around the safe confines of Fairfield, but with no working taillights, four bald tires, and an engine which consumed a quart of oil every hundred miles or so, his vehicle offered a poor choice for travel. Resourceful as ever, David Steiner convinced another local boy to rotate his tires onto R-O-D's dented Chevelle. Cross recalled, "When we put those other tires on they were just a bit too big. Consequently, I couldn't make very sharp turns without rubbing against the fender walls." On top of that, the car's heavy oil use worried the tiny driver. "I really wondered at the time if we would make it there." Still, the vehicle represented transportation and added to a sense of adventure. Reluctant parents watched the trio leave Fairfield just a day before the event was due to begin in upstate New York. Ahead lay the high-water mark of the American counterculture.

Driving straight through, the Wayne County natives arrived at the festival site in a mad rush. Dave Steiner's planning, however, had been so diligent that guards "were still taking tickets when we got there and there were still only a few cars." This calmness was quickly replaced by mass chaos as almost half a million people descended upon Woodstock, a crowd so large that promoters simply quit taking or selling tickets. Steiner had come totally prepared for the three-day event, or so he thought. Dave's family often camped, and the lanky Steiner had brought the family's large camping tent. But the advantages of this arrangement soon evaporated as it became clear that the privacy afforded by a tent was antithetical to the spirit of Woodstock. When Steiner returned to the tent at the end of the first day, he "discovered Rod Cross had invited thirty or so strangers to share the tent. When I asked him what the hell was going on he just grinned and said 'these are my guests.'" The disgusted Steiner, with no room in his own tent, grabbed a poncho and spent the rest of the time sitting near the front of the main stage. Kays and Cross spent much of their time at a smaller stage in an area called the Hog Farm. But the three young men found they did not need each other's company. Around them whirled a carnival like no other.

The Woodstock experience was certainly a profound one for nineteen-year-old Ken Kays. After living so long in the conservative community of Fairfield as something of an outsider, Woodstock both affirmed and empowered him. Later, during his short time in Vietnam, Woodstock was all he could talk about to anyone who would listen. "There's lots and lots and lots of us, more than anybody ever thought before," observed singer Janis Joplin. "We used to think of ourselves as little clumps of weirdos. But now we're a whole new minority group."[8] Terry Anderson, in his *The Movement and the Sixties*, noted that Woodstock was "destined to become the most famous event of the era, to live on in mythology." Eventually more than 400,000 people came to camp there. "As far as any one could see there were young people walking, lying down, drinking, eating, reading, singing. Kids were sleeping, making love, wading in the marshes, trying to milk the local cows and trying to cook the local corn. 'We were exhilarated,' one participant recalled. 'We felt as though we were in liberated territory.'" The youth quickly established "their own culture with their own rules, rituals, costumes, and standards of behavior. An observer noted that the cops were like 'isolated strangers in a foreign country,' and they made little attempt to enforce drug or nudity laws as the counterculture blossomed."[9] Perhaps the most important insight into Woodstock's impact on Ken Kays came from Duane Cornella, a New York native who, like Ken Kays, was always against the war but found himself being drafted after Woodstock and going to Vietnam, also like Kays. Cornella later commented, "I felt I was born that weekend."[10]

One can certainly speculate that Ken Kays' counterculture beliefs and antiwar stance were affirmed during those three days at Woodstock. Kays' later letter to his hometown paper, defending his sojourn there, would strongly reflect the Woodstock antiwar sentiments. "Wars have never led to peace, only to further wars," he asserted. Indeed, at Woodstock, the antiwar sentiment intertwined with the counterculture in a way that made the two indistinguishable. Michael Pridemore remembered how antiwar songs "got lots of cheers. We [at Woodstock] were an anti-war statement by our own example."[11] At Woodstock, the powerful presence of the antiwar position can be readily seen in songs such as Country Joe and the Fish's "I-Feel-Like-I'm-Fixin'-to Die Rag." The tune became something of an anthem for the antiwar movement, sarcastically telling parents to be the first on their block to bring their son "home in a box."

There was also a powerful dark side at Woodstock for those such as Ken Kays who tended toward addiction. Kays had been one of the very first in Wayne County to become involved in the pot scene, and he graduated to more powerful drugs while at Carbondale. Drug consumption was one of the major occurrences at Woodstock, and many there recall bad "trips" or being so stoned they have little memory of what went on. On Friday night a major announcement from the main stage warned of bad drugs, especially bad LSD. Brad Collins experienced one of the worst acid trips of his life there. "I was freaking out and people were trying to help me, but no one could do anything."[12] One concerned security guard remembered thinking, "This isn't a music festival—it's a drug convention."[13] That Kenny spent much of his time at the Hog Farm, where *Newsweek* reported the heaviest drug use of the entire festival, indicates a growing problem for the young man. Indeed, drug dependency would be a central aspect of Kays' adult life and came to be a major contributor to his death.

Not wishing to leave what had been a life-changing experience, the Wayne County trio lingered until almost everyone else had left. The place by this time looked like a battlefield without the bodies, with trash blowing to and fro or stomped deep into the mud. Steiner and Kays eventually found one another, but little Rod Cross was nowhere to be seen. Some years later Ken Kays told a Fairfield neighbor, "We were pretty worried. Almost everyone had left by this time. Then Dave and I saw something move way up the hill under a sleeping bag. I hollered, 'R-O-D, is that you?' Rod poked up from under the bag and waved."

When the three got to Cross's car for the trip home, they discovered two things—they didn't have enough money between them to buy the gas, oil, and food needed for the trip back to Fairfield, and Cross had lost his car keys somewhere at the Hog Farm. Luckily, the three Wayne County men discovered another trio—two girls from Canada and a young man from Minnesota—who agreed to help pay expenses to Illinois just for the adventure of traveling there. "The Minnesota boy knew how to hot-wire the Chevelle," Cross recalled, "and I was small enough to crawl through the hole, once we took out the back seat, to load our stuff up in the trunk."

But their adventures had not ended. While driving through Pennsylvania, a policeman pulled their vehicle over for having no working taillights. When Cross explained he'd lost his keys and had hot-wired the car, the policeman became even more suspicious of the six grubby-looking vagabonds. Cross recollected, "The cop's first remark was, 'You guys have been to that goddamn rock concert.' Fortunately the two girls from Canada who were with us kind of charmed the cop, and after we told him some things about Woodstock, he let us go." By the time Kays, Cross, and Steiner pulled into Fairfield, the nation, especially the more conservative general public, was already wrestling to digest what the Woodstock weekend might mean. In an article titled "Age of Aquarius," *Newsweek* magazine puzzled over it and disapprovingly observed, "At week's end near the Hog Farm campsite, a hard core of crazies barked like dogs and freaked out in a bizarre circle dance lit by flashing strobe lights. The songs seemed to sum up what the young Aquarians believed, despite all misadventures, the festival was all about: "Now, now, now is all there is. Love is all there is. Love is. Love."[14]

On Thursday, 21 August, an article written by David Steiner appeared in the *Wayne County Press*. The piece took up half a page and was headlined in big bold print "Fairfield Boy, Dave Steiner, Says New York Jazz Festival was the Wildest Week of His Life . . . 3 From Here Attend." In the lengthy article, a naive Steiner unintentionally related many things that would disturb the majority of Wayne County folks. Indeed, the young man's unvarnished report would most likely have shocked the older generation in any American community. Steiner told of "the wildest week I ever experienced." Steiner also related, "The costumes the visitors wore were in true Hippie fashion—wild colors—crazy outfits—long beards—headbands—you name it and it was there." The three Wayne County youths, according to Steiner, "visited a small lake in the area and saw over 300 guests swimming in the nude. Use of drugs among those present was quite common. They were smoking marijuana and consuming acid and speed pills without reservation. Drugs were being sold as openly as hot dogs at a baseball game." Asked if he tried any drugs himself, the young Steiner smiled at the *Press* reporter and remarked, "I smoked a little grass, but stayed off of that stronger stuff like acid and speed . . . they tell me it'll kill you in two years." Asked by the reporter if any of the group frowned on the use of drugs, he said not as far as he knew. "It's just accepted as part of the plan," he added.[15]

Before the Steiner interview ended, the *Press* reporter asked the young man if there was any use of drugs in Fairfield. Steiner's positive response dumbfounded the Fairfield community and started a firestorm of comments and letters to the local paper. Typical of the many letters which poured into the *Press*'s office was one in which the writer grumbled, "Mr.

Editor, How could you write an article on the hippies who went to the Jazz Festival? I could have cried when I read it. . . . I can't believe there are many of this type in Wayne County."[16] One writer even expressed her fear that the festival and the three Wayne County boys' participation in it was "all a part of the Communist plan."[17] In an open letter directed primarily at David but also indirectly to Ken Kays and Rod Cross, another concerned female wrote, "When I received the copy of your newspaper with the article on David's experience at the New York Pop Festival, I wanted to cancel my subscription. It is a terrible, lonely, miserable life to let Satan have such a strong hold on us, young or old whoever it might be. I feel so sorry for David. He is one identified with the so-called Hippie group. Who knows, maybe God will save you."[18] Greatly distressed by the many letters criticizing him and because of the complaints his parents were receiving, David Steiner penned a long, edgy, and facetious response to one female letter writer and to all the other critics who had been verbally attacking the trio since their return. In part, the irritated youth explained, "The August 21 article in the Press was not meant to shock rather to educate. I like Fairfield. I want the people to know to be aware. Try to understand we're all in this world together. What's it going to be like if we don't tolerate each other?"[19]

A young writer, who signed himself a "Fairfield Boy," also chimed in by attacking the hypocrisy of the community. Given the author's antiwar stance, it is likely the writer was Ken Kays, and in this letter we possibly find Kays' first public views on the war. He notes, for example, that wars never lead to peace but "only to further wars." The letter also offers valuable insight into Kays' attitudes about the many difficult issues of that day. The writer suggested that war resisters could be considered more courageous than those young men who were not really for the war but went to Vietnam anyway. "There are a number of double standards that exist in American society today. As the Vietnam veteran noted of the G.I. in Vietnam, 'Maybe he doesn't want to be there, but he is.' So because he is there, he is said to be a hero and super-patriot while the war protester at home who is against the war, just as the G.I. is, is said to be a bum. What is so heroic about fighting for something you don't believe in? Is a person who is deferred from the draft because of medical school or teaching any better American citizen than a conscientious objector who is deferred?" Concerning drugs, "Fairfield Boy" argued, "granted some of the stronger drugs taken by the hippies are quite dangerous, as Mr. Steiner pointed out in his interview, but they are no more dangerous than the liquor and beer sold by the bootleggers in Wayne County. I have seen men and women so intoxicated by liquor that they become dangerous to themselves and to others. Why haven't the 'interested parents' of Fairfield turned in the names of these bootleggers to protect the youth from being exposed to them? These bootleggers are far more numerous than the drug peddlers in Fairfield, rest assured."

In general, the astute young man blasted the conservativeness of his Wayne County audience. "Why was the rock festival so distasteful to you? Are your taste buds soured by a segment of our society enjoying their lives and living in peace and harmony? Would your appetite be whetted as the Vietnam veteran's evidently would by reading accounts of people killing and bleeding to death?" In summary, the young man, who was likely Ken Kays, observed, "The hippies did not form their society, they were formed by and from all of society. With the mess the world is in today, which is a result of mankind's societies through the ages, who can say the hippies are wrong? Wars have never led to peace, only to further wars. Why not try peace for awhile?"[20] Whoever the author, the letter indicates the kind of live-and-let-live view Ken Kays himself would later adopt.

Oddly enough, Steiner, Kays, and Cross found an ally in conservative reporter Jack Vertrees, who in his *Press* column "Random Thoughts" commented, "We'd like to step off the deep end. . . . There has been a flurry of letters criticizing both the Fairfield boys who went to the jazz festival and the *Press* for publishing an interview with one of the boys. Like we should stick our head in the mud and say it isn't so. Like we should continually write only that the world is one big happy family of love and friendship. Which would be a deception. And such deceptions are foremost among the items which have turned the young people off from the older generation." Vertrees went on to briefly explore the historical importance of Woodstock. "Three Fairfield boys going to a jazz festival, at which 300,000 or more took part. The festival made the national press, radio, and TV, so why not a local angle to this event?" As for the many letters inquiring why there were not more accounts about the "good" people of Wayne County, especially about those serving in Vietnam, Vertrees explained, "It takes all kinds of people to make up this world and tolerance of others is an attribute we should have more of."[21] Eventually, even the *Press* grew tired of the drama and announced in late September, "Two clippings in the anonymous mailbag, both directed to us for reading, dealing with the 'new morality of anything goes,' so prevalent at the Woodstock music festival. *We've had our say on that festival, will say no more.*"[22] Fairfield, however, would not soon forget the uproar.

Perhaps the most interesting bit of correspondence to come out of this heated debate was written by a combat-decorated Vietnam vet, Sammie Coplea. Coplea, a genuine hero who had received two Bronze Stars and two Purple Hearts, now bitterly complained to the editor of the *Press*, "I can't understand why the *Press* would send a reporter to interview a person who had attended a jazz festival. . . . From the article the young boy seemed proud of the fact he had tried marijuana. I fail to see why he was proud. I think it is disgusting that young people are exposed so freely to drugs, and then it is written up in an article and gives the intention that it is all right. I was in Vietnam and I have seen men so high on marijuana they couldn't think or act rationally. Doctors say it doesn't lead to stronger drugs; however, anyone who uses marijuana is very likely to try stronger drugs."

Coplea went on to grumble, "My main complaint is I have been to Vietnam and saw young men doing completely different things. I saw an 18 year old man bleed to death and plead with me for help. These young men are really doing their thing. Maybe he doesn't want to be there, but he is. When these young men come home to their families, on page 6 or 7 there is a short paragraph on his returning. Why doesn't the *Press* send a reporter to see him? His family is proud of him, and this would even make them more so. Maybe sending down a reporter to see him will make the year spent away from his loved ones seem worthwhile. I can't see why the *Press* wastes time interviewing a person who has attended a jazz festival and print it all across the top of the page when they could be interviewing young men the community should be proud of."[23] The rich irony of this particular letter is that one of the three hippie types the soldier so bitterly criticized would soon receive the nation's most prestigious award for military valor, the Congressional Medal of Honor.

5

Maybe I Can Help Somebody

In late summer of 1969, David Steiner, Joe Keoughan, and other friends of Ken Kays returned to their respective colleges. Meanwhile, Kays sat at home as national and world events continued to unfold and fashion his destiny. At first the news about the war and the draft seemed hopeful. Draft boards everywhere had begun to announce they would be cutting back on the numbers called in October. In late September, the *Wayne County Press* noted with some optimism, "The October draft call, according to Mrs. Mary J. Bullock has been cut from 11 to 4 for Wayne County, and that's good news. If we read the Nixon plan right, only about 11 will go from the county over the three month period of October, November, and December. Which will be good news for some lucky draft registrants who might have made up the call."[1]

In September, President Nixon himself declared, "The time has come to end this war." In his speech the president announced that 35,000 more men would come home by mid-December and that the numbers "could go higher."[2] Unfortunately, Kays and others in his situation were unaware of the president's political dilemma. Nixon's predecessor, Lyndon Johnson, had been politically destroyed by the war. After winning by a landslide in 1964, Johnson announced in March of 1968, after his acceleration of the war in Vietnam had turned the electorate against him, that he would not seek re-election. Now it was Nixon's turn in the hot seat. Indeed, it would only take a short while for the news media to switch from speaking of Johnson's war to criticizing Nixon's war.

Politically, Nixon could not simply pull out the troops. As he told one columnist at this time, "I'm not going to be the first president to preside over an American defeat." Nixon also declared, "The peace we will be able to achieve will be due to the fact that Americans, when it really counted, did not buckle, did not run away, but stood fast so that the enemy knew they had no choice but to negotiate."[3] In time, this position meant that more than twenty thousand more Americans would die as the United States struggled to disengage in Vietnam. Further, the division Kays would later serve with, the 101st Airborne, would receive the difficult task of maintaining heavy contact with the enemy as other American forces slowly stood down. Many astute leaders saw the darker possibilities of Nixon's stand of "peace with honor." Eugene McCarthy, for example, noted, "It's almost like we were back in 1966."[4]

In mid-October, less than a month after the exhilaration of Woodstock, Ken Kays received the news he had been dreading since flunking out at SIU. With fumbling fingers, he opened the letter addressed to him and quickly scanned the first line in disbelief: *The President of the United States, to Kenneth M. Kays. Greetings: You are hereby ordered for induction into the Armed Forces of the United States.* The words struck like a sledgehammer to the stomach.

Kays wasted little time seeking conscientious objector status through the local draft board. While the process seemed straightforward enough, determining CO status was a subjective process left in the hands of local draft boards and was thus subject to local norms and politics. Kays would seem to have had an advantage because of his parents' standing in the community, but by 1969 John and Ethel Kays' status in Fairfield probably carried less weight than their son's perceived antiauthoritarian behavior. Nevertheless, Kays hopefully filled out Selective Service Form 150, which required applicants to state whether they were requesting I-A-O status, which meant that they were willing to serve in the military in a noncombatant role, or I-O status, which meant that they were not willing to serve in the military in any capacity. Kays chose the latter status. The form also required applicants to write essays concerning "their reasons for requesting I-A-O or I-O status; the religious nature of their beliefs; the development of their beliefs from early childhood; and any public or private expressions of their pacifism." In reviewing the application, the draft board was to focus on the applicant's sincerity, "though in fact there was wide variation across the country in the draft boards' handling of CO applications."[5]

If the local draft board rejected the written application, as it did with Kays' request, the applicant could seek a personal appearance before the board. These interviews, conducted without attorneys, usually brought those seeking to avoid the war for philosophical or religious reasons in direct conflict with draft board members whose beliefs differed greatly from the applicant's. Given his exceptional intelligence, Kays' arguments were probably compelling. As friend Joe Keoughan indicated, Kays had been working out his antiwar beliefs for some time and in environments such as SIU that were conducive to developing serious and well-thought-out arguments against the war. But it was up to each local draft board to make the initial decision regarding draft status requests, and the Fairfield panel stood true to its traditional Midwest standards. To them, Kays' arguments simply failed to meet the criteria for conscientious objector status. There were other subjective considerations as well.

If letters to the editor of the local paper which followed Kays' and his two friends' visit to Woodstock were any indication, Fairfield's older generation had come to perceive Kays as a long-haired hippie type, which certainly placed great pressure on the board. A few adults, however, apparently thought otherwise. John Feldman, father of one of Ken Kays' friends, had written to the local paper the summer after the Woodstock controversy telling how Kays had been a Boy Scout and "a hard working student." Feldman also pointed out that young Kays, far from being some kind of hippie wimp, was in fact an extraordinary powerful person. The writer explained that the young man had "spent weekends and vacations engaged in mountain climbing and survival training," which he added "is probably the most he-man of all recreational sports." Of Kays' long hair, the writer argued that "this is a precedent set by such leaders of civilization as Ben Franklin, Isaac Newton, Albert Einstein, and, if we can believe the pictures, Jesus Christ himself."[6] Most in Fairfield, however, including the local draft board, failed to share Feldman's view.

The board may have also been influenced by the difficult times. By the fall of 1969, the nation had been moving in a more conservative direction in response to the antics of many of the younger generation, people like Ken Kays. Woodstock had become the primary embodiment of such goings-on, with antiwar demonstrations following close behind. News media reports exacerbated the problem. One activist in the antiwar movement lamented, for example, about how the media always seemed to focus on the most outrageous members in the antiwar groups.[7] There had also been the many complaints after the local Fairfield paper wrote of David Steiner's, Ken Kays', and Rod Cross's experiences at Woodstock. Clearly, the older generation in Wayne County and across the country now shuddered at the changes which exploded all around them as their beloved nation seemed to be falling apart. National media reports underscored this conservative swing. In October of 1969, as Kays struggled with the local draft board regarding his request for conscientious objector status, Newsweek carried a powerful and disturbing piece titled "The Troubled American." After taking extensive national interviews and polls, the article told how the so-called "silent majority" had become obsessed with "the hedonistic hippie and the campus revolutionary." The article went on to observe, "After years of feeling himself a besieged minority, America's vast white middle class majority is giving vent to his frustration, his disillusion, and his anger." Of particular concern to the older generation, according to Newsweek, stood the strange and scary behavior of America's young people.[8]

The huge October antiwar protest, the so-called Moratorium on the war, flared as a major national event, further upsetting the average American and perhaps further dooming Ken Kays' appeal. *Time* magazine warned, "Nixon cannot escape the effects of the anti-war movement." On the eve of the Moratorium, *Newsweek* carried a story, "Nixon in Trouble," and after the gigantic protest remarked that "there had never been a phenomenon quite like it." According to *Life* magazine, it was an event "without parallel, the largest expression of public dissent ever seen in this country."[9] The Moratorium shook the foundation of middle America, especially in places such as conservative Fairfield, Illinois. This can be illustrated by the reaction of one nearby local Illinois community leader when a young outsider came to his town to set up a Moratorium booth. His attitude was shared by a vast majority of Fairfield folks at that time, and his account further underscores the growing anger and fear the older generation now carried toward the young.

> This guy with greasy long hair and those granny glasses—a ridiculous-looking creep, I get mad just looking at them—anyway, he came into the township building, and he started setting up a card table and some signs. I got red. God, I got mad. I walked over to him and I didn't even read his sign. I knew what the hell he was all about. I said to him, 'What's your problem, pal? What's with you, pal?' I kept calling him pal every second breath, that's the way to keep those bastards off balance. I said to him, 'You ain't setting up nothin' like that in here, pal, let's get movin', pal.' Oh, hell yes, he started protesting, he was saying Nazi Germany and civil rights and freedom of speech and how I was no better than a German storm trooper, and I started getting madder. I reached out and grabbed him under my left arm—and got a good hold on him. . . . And I was holding him real tight, and he was hollering. And with my other arm—my right one, I picked up his lousy stinking card table and his goddamned sign and I pulled the whole mess right through the door and pitched his ass out on Water Street. 'Don't bring that sort of crap into this building, pal, and don't make me mad,' I told him. That's the only way to handle jerks like that—hustle 'em right on outside. I'm not letting any goddamned hippie jerk of a demonstrator use my office for that sort of thing.[10]

United States senator Ralph Smith spoke to a large crowd in Fairfield shortly after the huge national protests in October. His comments fell on fertile ground. The *Press* reported, "Declaring that the small minority of war protesters active in America today do not represent the view of the overwhelming majority, U.S. Senator Ralph T. Smith called on Wayne County voters to rally behind the President in a talk here Wednesday morning." Smith addressed a group of concerned county citizens at Robb's Coffee House. Noting the small American flag he was wearing on his lapel, the senator explained, "It is not just an accident that I happen to be wearing this flag this morning. I urge each of you this weekend to fly your flags . . . drive with your lights on . . . and let the protesters in Washington know that we are behind the President."[11] By 1969, the actions and antics of the counterculture had begun to cause a counterpunch of its own, with country and western music often catching its anger. Wayne County shops, grain elevators, truck stops, and country stores frequently played such tunes as Merle Haggard's "The fighting side of me," (1970) whose "America, love it or leave it" attitude summed up the way many in Fairfield felt about the antiwar point of view.

All things considered, Kenny Kays could not have chosen a worse time to approach the local draft board about seeking conscientious objector status. The David Steiner letter printed in the *Press* that summer, which had gone into delicious detail about the drug use and decadence at Woodstock, along with Woodstock itself and the Moratorium, greatly hurt Kays' chances. Nor did it help that the local paper was filled with articles about Wayne County servicemen receiving awards for valor, reports of wounds suffered, and in a few cases the deaths of local servicemen in Vietnam. Put simply, by the fall of 1969, the middle class wanted to strike back, and in Kays' instance they did. He would not get the deferment he sought.

Ken Kays now faced an agonizing decision. Denied conscientious objector status meant he could either enter the army or flee. The worried young man quickly looked up his best friend Joe Keoughan and asked him what he thought. Keoughan more than anyone else understood his friend's deep concerns about the war and recognized that Kays was not driven by fear. But the decision had to take into account other factors. Like it or not, Kays was a part of the Fairfield community, and in southern Illinois, that fact counted for something. "I told him I couldn't tell him what to do, but then added, 'I'll support you either way.'" Word soon got out that Kays was considering evading the draft.

To David Steiner, it seemed all of Fairfield now hounded Kays about going into the service. "Even my father pulled him aside and tried to use his influence to get Kenny to do his duty." Oddly, given his positive sentiments about his experiences at Woodstock, Steiner himself took no sides. "I was for the war, but having a college deferment, I felt it wasn't my place to say." Of great concern to Kays as well were the feelings of his parents. John and Ethel Kays stood as shining models of the World War II generation, and their hard work had brought them much respect in the Fairfield community. Rod Cross believed Kenny's fleeing would be especially hard on John Kays, given his service during World War II. Other key factors, however, eventually tipped the scales in favor of Kays' bolting to Canada.

Although many in the Fairfield area were solidly behind the Nixon administration, by late 1969, a large crack in support for the war had appeared in even such staunchly conservative places as Wayne County. America's rapid disengagement from the war could not be denied, and few wanted a precious son to be lost in a conflict from which we were soon to withdraw. By the time Kays came to struggle with being drafted, he could read of numerous reports in the *Wayne County Press* of local men who had gone AWOL from the army or fled to avoid the draft. In one instance parents took their two drafted sons with them to Mexico. Such outright opposition to the draft in the heartland of America indicated the growing level of concern about the war. Another force which may have influenced Kays was the size and energy of the national Moratorium in mid-October. Indeed, it was the largest mass demonstration against the war during our nation's involvement in Vietnam and could have only boosted Kays' own desires to strike out against the war. Kays also had a kind of cultural permission to take the drastic step of resisting authority because the region, as noted earlier, had a long history of antiauthoritarian sentiment. The not-so-secretly celebrated Shelton brothers, Charlie Berger, Blackie Harris, and small local bootleggers too numerous to mention were just a few of the cultural examples to which Kays could look. Finally, Kays knew of a network which could provide logistics for going to Canada. By the time Kays had entered SIU, for example, there were more than two dozen "we won't go" organizations on campuses. Further, *A Handbook For Conscientious Objectors* floated around at most major colleges and would have been accessible to the young Fairfield man.

As it turned out, Canada was a lonely and depressing place for Ken Kays. This aspect of his story can be better understood by looking at how fleeing to Canada impacted other young men like Kays. Many such accounts can be found in James Tollefson's *The Strength Not to Fight: Conscientious Objectors of the Vietnam War*. One midwesterner recalled of his situation, "Going in the army was completely out. I would have died there. . . . At first, Canada was out too. Canada was unknown in the Midwest. It was to me, anyway. I had hardly ever heard of the place." The other alternative was jail time. The desperate young man quickly went to see a counselor to talk about how to survive in prison. "He told me I'd probably end up in Leavenworth and would be raped the first week I was there. 'Oh great,' I thought, 'I can hardly wait.' Soon after that meeting, a friend casually asked, 'Why not go to Canada?' When I looked at the alternatives, it sounded like a pretty good idea." But then came the loneliness. "On the day I left, my older sister and my mother came with me to the bus station to say goodbye. My father couldn't come because he had to work. One of the images forever engraved on my mind is sitting on the bus and staring out the window, seeing my mother and my sister standing there, looking at me as the bus pulled away."[12] Another youth, a Californian, recalled thinking, "If I fled to Canada, I would never again be able to see the Redwoods, or the coast of California, or the other beautiful places that mattered so much to me, or the friends I had grown up with. And most of all, I would never be able to see my home again."[13]

Like many others who fled to Canada during the war, Kenny Kays would discover how much he belonged to the area from which he came. The cultural strength of his home region, southern Illinois, was especially potent. To add to his woe, while Kays struggled with tremendous bouts of loneliness, he received a call from his father, who begged him to come home. But John Kays offered more than just guilt to his only son. The elder Kays had been in contact with the army and had worked out a compromise he desperately hoped his son would accept. He would go into the army, but as a medic, and he would not have to carry a weapon. After a short month in Canada, the homesick Wayne County man reluctantly agreed to return to Fairfield. Rod Cross later offered a harsh assessment of what had taken place. "I think Kenny finally went to Vietnam because he didn't want his daddy to have to go to the coffee shop and deal with all the negative crap." Trying to make the best of a difficult situation, Kays told Cross that "maybe as a medic I can help somebody."

The difficulty Ken Kays faced during training for a conscientious objector army medic can be found in the accounts of other conscientious objectors at that time. One recalled, for example, how the experience was disturbing for conscientious objectors, who tended to be singled out for harsh treatment. "The platoon sergeants were especially hard on CO's. . . . It was like in concentration camps, where some inmates get special rank in order to keep order. The platoon sergeants took away my visiting privileges and my weekend passes. I was engaged at the time, and so I lost contact with my fiancee, who was my only emotional support." Medic training could also be short and could lack depth. "After basic, I went to Fort Sam Houston in Texas for medics' training. . . . Mostly, we learned how to make hospital corners on beds, give shots, and do IVs. Real minor stuff. Not much battlefield training. After only ten weeks, I got my orders for Vietnam. I remember the night before I left, sitting with an old friend, telling him how scared I was. He said, 'Have another beer.' Those were the days when a six pack could cure anything."[14]

Perhaps CO medic Steve Gunn's story serves as the best example of the conscientious objector training experience, given that Gunn was something of a free spirit himself and came to serve, like Kays, with the 101st in the spring of 1970. Like all army personnel instructed to be an army medic, Gunn was sent to Fort Sam Houston in San Antonio, Texas. Gunn's first memory upon coming into the base was of all the rocks which lined everything. "It was just like we had to have this sense of orderliness and everything had to be straight lines. From the beginning, the whole feeling of the training was us against them. . . . It was sort of like being a prisoner of war. First they cut off all your hair and then you have to run and do push-ups and calisthenics and when somebody of a higher rank is walking past you—you have to salute properly and if you don't they—you know, 'Drop and give me ten soldier.' Or twenty or whatever." Gunn also found it disturbing that no one had "any sense of mission about the war or anything." Gunn thought the medic training poor at best. "We sat in classrooms and practiced putting bandages on. We learned how to treat a chest wound, learned how to put in an IV, and take a pulse."

Kays likely would also have hated the regimentation which Gunn found almost unbearable. "Like in basic training, everything's regimented. And so you've got reveille and then you get up and you made your bed, you know, so a quarter can bounce on it, and then you have assembly and you all got out and everybody stands in line and reports in and then you stand in line forever to get breakfast and then you eat breakfast and then there's clean up time. You also had various chores and people are cleaning up the bathrooms right after breakfast." Worse perhaps were the fussy kinds of details found in the typical army training regiment. "The whole thing was set up as a break-you-down kind of thing. Your trash-waste baskets were never supposed to have anything in them. You had all of this stuff that you were supposed to have that you were never supposed to use. But it had to be in a little chest at the foot of your bed that had a particular order that it had to be in. They had things like you had a shaving brush, and shaving soap, and a razor, and nobody ever used shaving brush, shaving soap, or that razor, we just kept it there so it would always be clean and perfect when they came to do inspections. It was more of a sense of harassment. We just tried to maintain some degree of identity, and so I would listen to music. I was always listening to the blues, especially to Johnny Winter."

Ken Kays' own difficulties did not end after his basic and medic training. Sometime in March of 1970, John Keoughan recalled how Kays went AWOL while home in Fairfield on his thirty-day leave prior to leaving for Vietnam. "I told him he better go back right now. He just thought if he waited long enough they might come and say okay you're out." Finally Keoughan convinced Kays to return to the army. "But I also warned him I thought he'd likely be sent to a hot spot in Vietnam since he'd reported back late." Indeed, this would be the case. David Steiner remembered Kays' AWOL actions and thought to himself, "Well, that's just Kenny." Undoubtedly, Ken Kays stood as the last person in the world anyone from Fairfield, Illinois, would have imagined one day receiving the highest recognition for military valor.

Part II

Future years will never know the seething hell . . . the countless minor scenes of . . . war; and it is best they should not. The real war will never get in the books.

Walt Whitman

6

My Life Changed Forever

While Kenny Kays moved in fits and starts toward his unique destiny in Vietnam, a handful of other young American men who along with Kays would soon come to endure that hellish night on Fire Support Base Maureen found themselves on an unexpected journey, the destination of which remained painfully unclear. Their home cultures were vastly different, but the one thing they shared was the shadow of World War II. The so-called "good war" loomed over them in the form of their fathers' own service and in popular movies and television shows of that day that further enhanced the mystique of that war. Consistent with Kays' circumstances, when the time came for these young men to confront the possibility of going to Vietnam, the glorious accounts of their dads' generation blocked any real consideration of the war's importance or of whether or not to go.[1]

Gilbert "Gib" Rossetter came into the world on 20 July 1950, two years after Ken Kays' birth. A middle child with two brothers, Rossetter grew up in the supportive small-town atmosphere of Fowlerville, Michigan. Like Kays, the Michigan youth found some affirmation in sports, playing basketball and football and excelling at baseball. Also like Kays, Rossetter's father had served in World War II. As with most of his generation, the elder Rossetter kept oddly silent about his war experiences, adding an even more pronounced aura to that event.

Rossetter, as with other young men his age, grew more aware of events surrounding Vietnam as he approached his senior year in high school. "The Vietnam War was in the newspapers and on the television every night, and several of the kids from my hometown were going into the army or volunteering for other branches of the service. I had a few cousins, first cousins, that went in and ended up in Vietnam in '68 and '69. I was pretty proud of them, and the feeling generally around the school was 'Old so and so is over in Vietnam,' almost as if they were proud of him for being there. It really changed just two short years later."

As it had to Kays' community in Fairfield, Illinois, drugs and other features of the growing counterculture had also come to rural Michigan

Kenny Kays was a baby-faced twenty-year-old medic and conscientious objector who had been in Vietnam only two weeks when he helped save many of his 2nd Platoon comrades at Fire Support Base Maureen. Courtesy Randy Mills.

by the mid-sixties. "Drugs were just starting to come into my high school about my junior year in '66 and '67. It wasn't a part of my life so much or my friends' that I ran around with but it was certainly something that had not been there before." Still it was the war that drew most of Rossetter's attention. "I think a lot of us, at least in talking, would say that we'd like to get over to Vietnam, but I really didn't think that would even be a possibility for me, being a good student and a good athlete. I thought for sure I'd just be getting a 2-S and going on to college." Eventually, however, the war caught up with Rossetter despite his initial hope he would obtain a college deferment. "My plans on graduating from high school in 1968 was to go to Central Michigan University and play baseball. I was offered a scholarship my junior year in high school, although my senior year was a rebelling year for me. My coach and I didn't see eye-to-eye and I quit the baseball team my senior year in high school and lost my scholarship." At that time the young man decided that he would just work and "figure out where I was at." Obtaining a job in a factory that summer after high school, Rossetter soon bought a new car and "was pretty much living high on the hog. My friends I had gone to high school with went on to college, and I was classified 1-A. I was making money, and they were spending their parent's money at school. I was also going with a girl. I had been going with her for about three years. I wasn't sure where that relationship was going. So I went into

Tough South Side Chicago native Steve "Greek" Avgerinos. His cool thinking and actions during the Fire Support Base Maureen melee aided greatly in 2nd Platoon's desperate fight on 7 May. For his role in the battle, Greek received the Bronze Star with "V" device. Courtesy Steve "Greek" Avgerinos.

the draft board in December of '68 and asked them when they thought I'd be drafted and they told me probably in June or July. So I volunteered for the draft and went in on February 14th of 1969."

Not too many miles away in distance but light-years away in culture, another young American youth, Steve Avgerinos, struggled to come to grips with his own adolescence and with the possibility of being drafted. Destined to be called "Greek" by his comrades in Vietnam, Avgerinos grew up in a tough neighborhood in Chicago, where he developed a savvy that would enable him to carry out great acts of bravery on Fire Support Base Maureen in May of 1970, feats which would bring him the Bronze Star with "V" device for valor along with a Purple Heart. Of his difficult adolescence and of being drafted, Avgerinos recalled, in the simple straight-forward style of the South Side, "I was born April 27, 1949, and raised on the south side of Chicago. I was one of eight kids, four boys and four girls, with an Irish Catholic mother and a Greek father. I was pretty sure I would be going into the army since I was the right age, eighteen, my draft number was 13, and college was not an option." At that time Avgerinos held mixed emotions about Vietnam. "A big part of me wanted to do the right thing for God and country because anything less would have been cowardly. Another part of me was scared because I knew of at least two guys from the old neighborhood that graduated a year ahead of me, and they had already come back in body bags."

Enlisting before he was drafted, the young Chicago man was sworn in just after Thanksgiving Day in 1968. Avgerinos received his indoctrination into the army at Fort Leonard Wood, Missouri. "It was nothing special, just the same screaming and dehumanizing treatment that everyone got in basic training back then." Advanced infantry training came at Fort Lewis, Washington. "My MOS [military occupational specialty] was 11C [mortar man]. I originally thought this was good because only 11Bs got sent to the field in Vietnam." It was during this phase of the young man's preparation that he received news of his first cousin's death in Vietnam. "To this day I still don't know all the details. I remember that we had a night exercise the day I was told. It sticks in my memory so well because we were issued limited blank ammunition and the training instructor said that in order to make it authentic we should make the sound 'pow-pow' like rifle firing if we ran out of ammunition! His statement was so ludicrous on top of my cousin's death that I was crying and laughing at the same time. I guess it must have made sense to him though because everyone did refer to the M-16 as a Mattel toy. I didn't go home for his funeral though because I thought I might go AWOL."

Way down in west central Alabama lay the tiny communities of Sumiton and Dora, in a region where the primary livelihood was coal mining. It was in this sometimes idyllic, often difficult, small-town environment that Greg Phillips was born on 22 August 1948. Like so many of his generation, Greg's father fought in World War II. The elder Phillips had been "just a boy" when he was drafted out of Dora High School in 1942, but the son recalled that his father hardly ever talked about his war experiences. The younger Phillips lived in a dual world, witnessing the often abject poverty of the coal-mining towns while at the same time being insulated from its harsher aspects. "In high school and most of my school years, I was always one of the lucky ones. Most kids' dads were coal miners or some other blue-collar job. My dad was a sales rep for H.J. Heinz Company. He worked there for twenty years, and that's what got me into the business when I got back from the service."

Life was good for Phillips in those innocent times, especially during those warm summer evenings when Alabama kids drove their own version of the Fairfield, Illinois, "circuit." Phillips remembered, "Each Saturday night the place to be and the place to be seen was Sherer's, a really neat drive-in that sat just above the post office in Sumiton. Most everyone would just park in front and watch the muscle cars go by, or if you had money for gas you could be one of the circling cars. Gas was only twenty-five cents per gallon back in the sixties, but most everyone would just sit in their cars or their buddies' cars and watch."

Phillips' parents also saw to it that their son would come to understand the harsher aspects of the world. "My Grandfather Phillips was a miner and my mom's dad, Grandfather Griffin, ran the company stores for several mining companies in Alabama. When I was a teenager I worked in one of these company stores one summer and saw how hard these people worked and how the company treated them. I realized that I would never work for a company like this company nor would I ever treat people like they treated them." Perhaps it was Phillips' mother who most imparted to the young man the fierce drive that would enable him to rise up from the relative safety of his foxhole on 7 May 1970 and go to the heart of that ghastly struggle. His brave actions there would bring him the Silver Star and a Purple Heart. "My mom was the one who molded me and made me a hard charger. This attitude probably caused me to have the two heart attacks before I was forty-three." Too busy with school assignments and working at the local grocery store, Phillips never participated in sports, but the hard-working, get-things-done Phillips found himself chosen president of the student council in junior high and president of the steering committee in high school, a position equal to president of the senior class. Phillips' mostly pleasant world ended abruptly, however, when he was drafted almost immediately after graduating from the University of Alabama. He had been married for only three weeks to his high school sweetheart, Krystal.

Far from the summers of the Deep South, up in the cold regions of New England where locals claim there are two seasons—August and winter—Richard "Dick" Doyle grew to young manhood in the ruggedly picturesque town of Bellows Falls, Vermont. Born on 6 September 1945, Doyle would be one of the "old" men when destiny later brought him to the 101st Airborne. Doyle's father, Edward Doyle, had served in World War II as had other family members, and the elder Doyle came back from the Pacific theater telling stories of his experiences on a PT boat. The Doyles were devout Irish Catholics, perhaps more so than Dick Doyle realized as a youth. Upon his safe arrival from Vietnam, for example, he learned his mother had "burned votive candles for me the entire time I was there. I found this out when I returned home. She didn't want to jinx me by telling me while I served. She saved every empty container and showed them to me on my return."

Upon graduating from high school, Doyle attended the University of Vermont. The first year there he found that ROTC was mandatory as the school was a land grant college. The university dropped it as a requirement in 1964, but the specter of possible military service did not vanish. Like so many others after 1968, Doyle was drafted soon after graduation from college. The event came as a great shock, especially since the young Vermont man had already come to see the war as a tragic waste. "I spent much of my college years getting by, kind of avoiding the draft like most college males. I listened to and watched newscasts often about the Vietnam War, so much that I became desensitized like much of the public. I remember distinctly the weekly body counts and wounded reports on newscasts, but I stayed ambivalent as long as it didn't affect me. By the time I was drafted in 1969, my strong personal feeling was that the war was a lost cause, a bottomless pit sucking up money and young lives with little progress. As it turned out, the date of my being drafted, 7 May, would also later come to have a double significance for me. There seemed to be a major disconnect between what Washington was saying and energy and intensity that VC/NVA [Viet Cong/North Vietnamese Army] were showing. I didn't want to go to war, but knew I would if drafted and fate took me there. It did." In retrospect, Doyle's experience after being drafted served as a watershed event in his life. "I grew up about tenfold during my military and war experience. I was an irresponsible excuse maker in college, and the military changed all that."

Looking back, Doyle's memories of his youth before being drafted were, like so many who came to serve alongside Ken Kays in Vietnam, conflicting ones. "I started high school in 1959 (Bellows Falls High School), graduated with a class of ninety-eight in 1963. I was vice president of my class in junior and senior years. I played track and some football—usually small-town stuff, hanging out with friends. Back then my family aspired to have me go to college. My older brother started college in 1961. I was a bright but lazy student so I had to go to a prep school, Vermont Academy, in order to get into college at the University of Vermont. High school was difficult, as I was shy with girls and my mother and father were slowly breaking up." All in all, Doyle recalled, "living in rural Vermont in a town of 3,000, life sure wasn't all that complicated. That would come later."

Perhaps the most unlikely hero of the group destined to fight for their lives on 7 May 1970, besides Kays, was diminutive and quiet Kenneth David, who grew up in Girard, Ohio, near Youngstown. Born to an ardent Catholic family in 1950, the soft-spoken young man, known as "Little David" in Vietnam, stood barely five foot five and weighed just 140 lbs. by his senior year in high school. A four-year high school band member, where he played the drums, the soft-spoken David took a $2-an-hour job with the Ohio Department of Transportation upon graduation. "I bought a nice car and, by living at home, had a pretty nice life at the time. My family was blue-collar, my father a machinist, so I thought I was doing good at the time." The war in Vietnam was going strong in 1968, the year Ken David graduated from Girard High School, but the young man gave little thought to the possibility he might be drafted. Fate, however, intervened. In 1969, "a friend of mine enlisted in the marines and tried to get me to sign up also. A week after I took him to the bus station I got drafted. I reported to Cleveland, was bussed to Fort Campbell, Kentucky, and then to Fort Polk, Louisiana, and finally off to Nam." Drill instructors likely wondered what kind of soldier the small, quiet young man would make. Ironically, despite his size and gentle demeanor, Ken David's actions on the night of 7 May 1970 would bring him the second highest award for military valor, the Distinguished Service Cross.

For Ken Kays and his future comrades, fortune conspired to bring them together into the bleakest period of the conflict in Vietnam, the portion of the war fought after 1969. Fate also brought them to the 101st Airborne Division, not the best fate if one hoped to escape combat. The efforts of troops in the 101st, the "Screaming Eagles," in Vietnam after 1969 make for an important case study of this often neglected and misunderstood portion of the war. The division had proved to be one of the more successful units in the conflict and had a proud reputation prior to late 1969. Following the hard-fought battle on Hamburger Hill in May of 1969, however, things changed dramatically for the division. After 1969, the majority of the troops arriving into the Screaming Eagles' ranks were now basic-issue draftees—replacement troops rather than professionals. These draftees had not been immersed into the 101st's aggressive military traditions, and certainly none of them wanted to be the last man killed in a war the U.S. was no longer fighting to win. These two aspects could be readily seen. A 101st historian at the division's headquarters at Fort Campbell, Kentucky, said he could take old photos of 101st men who were serving in Vietnam, place them in a box, shake the box, and randomly pull out photos and always be able to tell the pre-1969 group from the post-1969 group. "The lack of professionalism of those who served after '69," noted the army historian, "was that glaring."

John Smith, a 101st lieutenant who served as a leader for Kays' platoon after that bloody night in May of 1970, believed, in this same regard, that "by 1970 the 'kick ass' attitude of the 101st Airborne Division was only present in the 'lifers.' By and large, the line troopers were poorly motivated. After all, it was no big secret the war was over, so who wants to be the last one to die in Vietnam?" All in all, the situation confronting those 101st men out in the field after 1969 could drive even the strongest mad.[2]

Gib Rossetter vividly recalled his training after being drafted and his ensuing journey to Vietnam. In February of 1969 the young Michigan man ended up at Fort Bragg, North Carolina, for basic training. "I took all the tests and scored pretty high and was given several options of re-enlisting for another year to get the MOS of my choice. But I could tell after the first few weeks in the army that I wanted to get out as soon as I could. I didn't like that spit-and-polish and the ordering around that I was getting. I could just tell that the military was not for me." Oddly, Rossetter had little fear about going to Vietnam at that time, although he calculated he would probably end up there. "I've always been a survivor and thought that

I'd survive Vietnam also. I was at Fort Dix for eight or nine weeks for my advanced infantry training."

Two weeks before graduating from AIT, the commanding officer called ten men, including Gib Rossetter, into his office and informed the trainees "he had six allocations for NCO school. He said the way he had it figured out, that we'd be at NCO school for twelve weeks and we could get other training and you'd stay in country for at least the first year service time, and the war was winding down at that time, and that he didn't think we'd ever end up in Vietnam. So my hand shot up." But the promise of escape from Vietnam did not come to pass. "The six of us got our orders on graduation day for NCO school at Fort Benning, Georgia. As it turned out, the rest of the company that I was in got orders for Germany. I'd love to talk to some of those guys that I was in AIT with that went to Germany and see if they ever ended up in Vietnam, but I suspect they probably didn't. And I've always been told 'don't volunteer for anything in the service,' and you know, you always think—they make it sound so good. So I volunteered and I ended up in Vietnam."

When Rossetter received orders for Vietnam, he also obtained a thirty-day leave. "I went back up to Michigan, and at that time and I was pretty proud that I was going to Vietnam. I felt good about myself. I felt good about my training." Rossetter's mortar designation helped ease his worries about enduring combat. "I had talked to one of my cousins who was in mortars, and he spent most of his time at a base camp in the rear. He said he felt pretty safe all of the time. So I felt pretty good about my situation going over to Vietnam at that time." While on leave in his hometown, the proud soldier returned to basketball games at his old high school. At one of these, the novice soldier came face to face with the powerful antiwar feelings that had swept the nation. "I went down in between halves to get a Coke and popcorn or whatever, and I was standing at the concession stand talking with a couple of my friends and I got pushed from behind. And I turned around and this young man that was probably about three or four years younger than myself pushed me, and he said 'I hear you're going over to Vietnam.' And of course the chest went back out and I said 'I sure am.' And he said 'The war's wrong' and he was just really pretty loud and obnoxious and I pushed him back and slammed him into the wall and grabbed his shirt collar and was getting ready to just paste him right in the face, and my arm got held up by one of the teachers. He broke us apart." Later, Rossetter's antagonist became one of his best friends. "Turned out the kid's name was Keith Dietrich and another year and a half later, I was living with him when I got home. Keith became one of my best friends, the best man at my wedding in '75. He was just ahead of my time when we clashed at that basketball game."

Oddly, the young Michigan man now found himself eager to get to Vietnam. "I felt that I was prepared pretty well by the service. Especially that four-week course after jump school with the survivor training." Conversely, Rossetter's parents were anything but eager for their son to go to war. "I think my dad—hearing a little bit about his own service history—he understood that this was not going to be a walk in the park. As they say, war is hell, but actual combat is a son of a bitch. And I think my dad knew that and understood that." The son tried to ease the worry his parents might have by writing letters home from Vietnam that simply did not indicate what was really occurring, but the ploy failed with the elder Rossetter. "He didn't believe what I was saying in the letters, because I did tell him when I got over there that they put me in an infantry company. I'd write my parents letters—everyday I would write home and tell them, you know, no action. In most of them I said I was back in the rear in our base camp, Camp Evans, partying and whatever and that I was seeing no action. My mom, I think she was naive enough to believe that. And that's probably what made her survive that year that I was there."

Vermont native and future 2nd Platoon member Dick Doyle also endured the rigors of basic training and the dreaded possibility of going to Vietnam. "My basic training was at Fort Dix, New Jersey, and right after the drill sergeant, Harty, took control of us he got us outside our company area and put us through a full-blown physical fitness test. I wasn't in very good shape as I had partied quite a bit before being drafted. I did the shuttle run, the horizontal bars, the man carry, and just finished the low crawl through a pit of sand and was at the far end, vomiting into the cinder blocks that lined the jogging track. I was laying on the ground feeling sorry for myself when I saw a pair of boots close to my face." The drill sergeant asked the sickened Doyle, "'Are you almost done, because you've got to run a mile now.' I couldn't believe it! Then and there, I knew my life had changed dramatically. I got up, held my aching stomach and side, and ran a mile at basically a snail's pace, but I made it."

One upsetting event the Vermont man especially recalled occurred part way through training. "We were involved with bivouac and war games, and a group of soldiers in my platoon were taking pictures of each other with a machine gun and bands of machine gun ammunition blanks crisscrossed over their chests with their gear and helmets on, looking like a bunch of John Waynes." Doyle asked them why they were bothering with such macho behavior. "They told me they were National Guard soldiers, that after basic training they were going back home until it was time for them to do their advanced training. Depressing!! I thought everyone was in the same boat I was in, but not so. At some level I hated them because they had taken a different and obviously easier path."

During Doyle's advanced infantry training at Fort Lewis, Washington, the first troop withdrawals from Vietnam were announced by President Nixon. "We were upbeat about that for awhile. Little did we know how long that process would be drawn out. In the first few weeks of training they asked for volunteers to go to NCO school at the end of AIT, an extra six weeks of training, so I volunteered, figuring if I postponed going to Vietnam anything could happen. I got turned down and that really bruised my ego. In hindsight it was a good thing as it would have altered my time line in Vietnam which could have had disastrous results." By 1970, the army going to Vietnam was made up almost entirely of draftees. Doyle's unit, for example, "was composed of about 90 percent draftees and the rest enlisted, and none of us had any doubt as to where we were headed next."

As time passed, Doyle knew he would soon be leaving for Vietnam. A letter from his brother did not help Doyle's plunging mood. "My brother sent me a great letter about an awesome rock concert he went to in New York, with more people than he could imagine—Woodstock. The closer we got to graduation, the more foreboding our mood became as we knew what was next. I graduated in September and got a two-week leave and headed home. Nixon had announced troop withdrawals, and it was a cause for elation temporarily, but at a more sophisticated level it meant that the war was a lost cause and that domestic political pressure was beginning to steamroll." To Dick Doyle, it meant "why should or would a soldier want to go and fight a war that the president just announced we were beginning to remove ourselves from? The only answer could be that you had to! So that was my mindset as I was completing training and awaiting orders for Vietnam. To me, at that juncture, it became a war not to die in."

Doyle remembers his flight to Nam as particularly peculiar. "Shortly after the plane took off, we stopped briefly in Alaska and Japan, I delved into a writing frenzy that was remarkable. I began writing everyone of importance in my life, including a couple of ex-girlfriends, in a clearing-the-air type of fashion that amazed me. I was practically in a trance. I'm sure I was putting words to paper in case I never was heard from again and/or never returned. It was one of the most cathartic experiences of my life." Doyle also wanted to pen his friends and family so that once in Nam, he could forget them and concentrate all his energies on survival. "That part of my plan I did to perfection. I wrote very little while I was in Vietnam, mostly done out of guilt, so family would know I was alive. Thinking of family and friends as a distraction sounds cold and calculating, but it's what I had to do." Conversely, Doyle's father, a World War II veteran, would write his son "at least five times a week. They were very low-key letters, but the thought of him writing meant more than the words."

Strong-willed Alabama native Greg Phillips found his initial training surreal. "All the attention at Fort Benning was focused on landing on the moon. For an entire week we stayed in the induction center while everyone watched stuff about the moon landing." Basic training for Phillips was typical for the time. As always, however, the possibility of being chosen for Vietnam hung over them like an axe. "The key event occurred toward the end of basic. If you were chosen to shoot at the range with an M-16 rifle, you were in deep, deep trouble. That means you were chosen for Vietnam. I always kept a very good attitude, thinking that I wouldn't be one of these guys that was picked for this." A week before basic training was over, Phillips was chosen as part of the one-third that was picked to go to the range and qualify with the M-16 rifle, "which was not a good omen. I had a friend that worked with the company clerk in the office and about two days before we were to graduate from basic training, he came to me and said, 'Well,' he said, 'I've got bad news for you, Greg. You are going in the infantry.' My world was crushed. I couldn't really believe that was going to happen to me. But, lo and behold, once I graduated from basic training, I found myself on a bus the very day of graduation, that evening, headed for Fort Polk, Louisiana, for eight weeks of AIT, advanced infantry training."

Ken David's story of training and early Vietnam experiences is chronicled in a number of letters the quiet but dedicated young man sent home to his family back in Girard, Ohio. While in training at Fort Polk, Louisiana, in early 1970, David told of the Mickey Mouse things which sometime occurred. In one instance he reported, "The reason I didn't call today is this: One of the men lost his M-16 weapon, and we were all restricted to the company area. We came in from Tiger Ridge Friday morning but they took a group back out to the ridge to see if they could find it. They didn't come back until 3:30 the following morning. Then all day Saturday they looked for the missing weapon wall to wall. They did foot-locker inspections and everything to try to find it. There were more generals walking around here than you would believe. They were watching us like hawks, and if anyone left the area and got caught, they suspected that person of taking it. They think one of us took it so they are watching every move we make. So that's what happened."

David described his flight to Vietnam in a 30 January 1970 letter. "Well, I'm on my way over. My plane left at 9:00 P.M. It's 12:30 A.M. right now and only 10:00 P.M. Hawaii time. That is my first stop. The plane will be there to take on food and fuel. It will only be there about one hour. It's hard to just sit here and think about home. I saw my first movie on an airplane. My ride will be between twenty-two and twenty-four hours long but they try to take your mind off things. They had a show, passing out books and writing paper, soft drinks, food, and we have our own music—we wear earphones. We can turn them to the music we want to hear, anything from jazz to old people's music." The concerned son also told his family, "Just take care of yourselves and don't worry too much. I can take care of myself. It's just hard on everyone, but the homesickness will leave sometime. So tell everyone I miss them already, and I'm thinking of them. Take care and tell the kids to behave."

After his arrival in Vietnam, the homesick Ken David quickly wrote from the 101st Division base at Camp Evans. "How is everything back home? Is everyone OK? How's Dad's cold? Is he better? I hope so. Well here I am. I'm over here. I'm a day ahead of yours back home where you are. It is only the 16 Feb 70, 7:00 P.M., so as I write this and just starting my day, you are all just finishing your day." David went on to describe his new surroundings. "The weather over here is wet right now. It's at the end of the rainy season. I have been here twenty days already and seen the sun only about seven times, but when the sun does come out, boy, does it get hot. Well, I want to get some sleep, so tell everyone I said 'hi' and I will try to write everyday now to let you know what happens."

Most of Ken David's early correspondence purposely ignored the hardships of Nam, especially combat, and concentrated on happenings back in the world. In one early letter, for example, the homesick youth asked, "How is everything back home? Everything is fine with me." He then went on to note, "For the last two nights I pulled guard at night, and they let me sleep in the morning till dinner time, so it wasn't too bad. I was supposed to have it tonight, but they had enough so I was lucky tonight. It rains almost every day and there's that damp smell all the time." The Ohio native especially appreciated the closeness he found in the 101st Airborne Division. "The men down here are OK. This is like one big family. Everyone looks after one another and that's the way it has to be over here." Not being able to keep his thoughts from home for long, the gentle son soon returned to his favorite theme. "How's Dad's cold? Is he better? How are the kids? Tell them I said 'hi' and to be good. You are probably just eating supper right now on the 17th of February. What are you having? I bet it was good. Do you mind if I come home to get some good food? I wish I could. Pretty soon I will. When I get done with this. I'm going to get some sleep. Just think, I've been here 21 days already. It doesn't seem like it. The days are going fast. It's only been 23 days since I left home. It seems like only yesterday. Tell everyone I said hi and I'll try to write. Well, I'll finish for now. So, take care, and I'll be waiting for some mail. Probably you were waiting also. So, goodnight. On the other page I said you are having supper. I made a mistake. You are just getting up to get Dad and the kids to work and school. So, have a good day."

The environment described by David seemed almost idyllic and suggested there was little fighting for the 101st. But there were hints of darker occurrences. In one letter he relates, "Well, I'm out in the field now. I came out yesterday afternoon. I'm in the 2nd Platoon in the Mortar Squad." Still, David liked the new outfit to which he now belonged. "I was lucky to get into it. Everyone in the platoon is a real bunch of good guys. They try to help us new guys out as much as possible. They have a nickname for all new guys. They call us 'Cherries' because we're new in the country." Not too smoothly, the letter shifts from picturesque to ominous. "We're on top of a hill right now and can see for miles around us. It's real quiet and peaceful. The guys all have suntans. It's hard to believe that I'm in a war zone. During the day there is helicopter noise and at night there are crickets and frogs, and of course we pull our guard around our camp. At night about five or six we go out on an ambush. I went out last night. It's no big thing. They do it every night. They go out and pick a spot on the side of a trail and wait for anything to come down and then ambush them."

As Ken David's correspondence suggests, when those involved with the 101st came to Vietnam in early 1970, they found themselves involved in a war mostly without front lines, with small patrols being sent out occasionally on search-and-destroy missions. But these smaller engagements often exploded into some of the fiercest fighting of the war, especially after March of 1970. John Smith, a lieutenant with the 101st who would later take over Kays' 2nd Platoon after the debacle of 7 May, recalled this difficult portion of the war and how fluid the fighting circumstances could be. "When we were preparing for a mission it usually occurred on short notice. Our general method of operation was to deploy in battalion strength around a fire support base, which as the name implies provided artillery support for the units patrolling the area. If a unit should initiate contact with the enemy, the commanders could then develop the situation as they saw fit. In theory, the unit in contact would attempt to maintain the engagement until reinforcements could be brought to bear to trap and destroy the enemy. We never went looking for supplies really. Most of the time the encounters were small, brief, and violent. So, in the sense that we were looking for the enemy, a mission would generally start with a meeting at the company CP, or a radio instruction for a platoon to move in a certain direction to attempt to locate the enemy."

John Smith, as a good platoon lieutenant would, wrestled with trying to follow difficult orders while at the same time attempting to get his young charges home alive and in one piece. In this difficult process the kind-hearted Smith grew much aware of the sufferings, both minor and extraordinary, the men of 2nd Platoon came to endure. Perhaps the greatest terror endured by Ken Kays' platoon and other 101st soldiers involved night activity in the field. John Smith recalled, "As to what the nights were like; in short, they sucked. You humped around all day, and usually tried to move into an NDP [night defensive position] just before dark, in hopes that the dinks weren't following too closely. You dug holes for indirect fire protection and to use as fighting positions if needed. There was a trade-off there. If you moved into your night defensive position too early, Charlie could see where you went, but you could dig in deep to make him pay if he decided he wanted to mess with you. However, if you wanted to hide really well, you could move into position late, but since noise travels much further in the dense night air, you had to forfeit the security of dug-in protection." Mostly, Smith recalled how he and his men "just sat there listening to the sounds of the jungle, no shelter or poncho tents, etc. If it rained, you sat or slept in the rain. If it was hot, you tried to keep the mosquitoes away without smelling up the AO [area of operations] or slapping too loudly. Add that to the suspicion that there were bad guys out there who possibly knew exactly where you were, and every shadow or sound becomes a man in your mind's eye. Day combat is scary, but night combat has to be absolutely terrifying."

All in all, the young southeast Missouri native found the situation in the 101st's area of operation especially disturbing in the early part of 1970. "I was career-oriented but quickly found that none of my troops were. I was struck by so many impressions, some very conflicting. The men were so young, you couldn't help but notice that." Smith also discovered the will to fight only existed with "the 'lifers,' that is, field grades, senior NCOs, and a few company-grade officers. By and large the line troopers were poorly motivated on their own. After all, it was no big secret that the war was over, so who wants to be the last one to die in Vietnam?"

Of significant impact upon those who served in Vietnam after 1969 was the increasing sense of the war's absurdity. The multiplying confusion about the necessity of the war can be seen, for example, in the increasing number of "white dink" sightings after 1969. So-called white dinks were foreign fighters, some even thought to be AWOL American soldiers, who supposedly went over to the enemy. The possibility of their existence would reach the level of folklore and legend before the war ended. As the conflict moved to its final bleak stage, claims of spotting such fighters increased. Although little or no official documentation can be found as to the actual existence of such combatants, Keith Nolan, in his book *Ripcord*, noted at least two such sightings by mid-1970. Personal letters of 101st Airborne members also reported the possibility of Anglo-looking enemy fighters whom the writers assumed to be Soviets. 101st trooper Kurt Maag, a Californian, and his platoon, however, had an actual encounter with a likely American serving alongside the enemy.

"We were following an old highway in open country," Maag recalled. "Visibility was quite extensive. I heard someone yell 'BANG' up ahead somewhere and to the right of us. No shots were fired however, so we continued on." As Maag's platoon filed through a place where the roadway squeezed between "steep rising cliffs to our left and a bit of the mountain forest to our right, mostly bamboo grove, a guy yelled 'BANG! You're Dead!'" It was at this point Maag witnessed the unbelievable.

"A white guy and two dinks were crouched behind a chi com [Chinese communist] machine gun. The dinks, both in NVA uniform, carried AKs [the AK-47 assault rifle was the standard weapon of the VC/NVA]. All three weapons trained on me. Their position, well-concealed from the road and reinforced with bags, was only visible from the point where I stood. So the rest of the platoon had no idea what was up except this guy shouting, my stopping dead in my tracks, and no shots being fired." The American enemy did not move or talk at first but just seemed to stare into Maag's eyes more intensely as the time passed. Maag recalled, "He was blond, blue-eyed, rather thin, and was dressed in GI gear. I'd say his accent was southern and he seemed to be scared almost as much as I was."

Maag was caught dead to right. The rest of the strung-out platoon was not in a good position either. "Our guys had little cover and really only one way to go, right into the enemy's entrenched fire, if it came to it." Something, however, in the demeanor of the turncoat American eased the initial tension. "Don't really know how to explain it, but within a few seconds of making eyeball-to-eyeball contact with this guy, I felt that he had no wish to fight us at all. He swung the machine gun around to his left, once I had taken my own finger off the trigger of my weapon. I came to sort of a one-handed port arms, and put my heels together to face him." The 101st platoon leader quickly came up to assess what was occurring. "Our lieutenant, having only heard the guy, not able to see anything except me stopping cold in my tracks and then straightening up rather stiffly, wanted to know what was going on. I gestured with my M-16 where the dinks were and the American. The white dink began speaking something about 'Do you want to fight or do you want to talk?' The white guy had turned the machine gun towards the center of our column, where the lieutenant and the radioman were. One of the dinks with him kept his AK trained on me just in case I suppose."

Maag's lieutenant radioed in that the platoon had had contact, "but apparently when he reported what was happening, the battalion commander had no interest in talking, he wanted bodies. Throughout this brief period when the lieutenant was on the radio, the white dink was haranguing him and the rest of us, and the situation started tensing up. About this time another dink revealed himself, standing in heavy camo just at the edge of the heavy forest growth, a bit behind the trench the white guy and two dinks were occupying." Maag could see the new enemy was a sniper. "He was heavily camouflaged with foliage hanging on him like the dinks would on the mountains. The lieutenant wisely chose not to fight." As the 101st platoon cautiously passed the now-exposed enemy, "Some of the dinks just laughed and even waved as our column moved along the road. It had probably only been three to five minutes but it seemed like hours."

Steve Avgerinos's arrival in Vietnam brought him almost instantly into the bitter and confusing war Smith and Maag described. The young man, who became known simply as "Greek," recalled, "My welcome to Nam was early on when Captain Skinner's RTO got killed. His name was Paul Frink. I was on the radio for our platoon when all hell broke loose. Someone told me later on that they were pretty well screwed because they hadn't dug in, and the explosions and screaming pretty well confirmed it at the time. It was pretty unnerving for someone who wasn't in country that long." The Chicago native carried the dead trooper the next morning in a poncho stretcher. "I remember feeling guilty because I was tired and angry that a guy I just met was dead already and that he was so heavy." Other more difficult events lay ahead for Avgerinos. "On one occasion we moved through some flat lands and up a rise. When we walked the extended perimeter for our night position, we didn't go too far because of the cliff on one side. We received a visit that night and Lt. Fletcher responded immediately. He had us lay down fire and called in for air support. He needed a volunteer to hold up the strobe light and without thinking of the exposure I took it. The next day we discovered that they had been dug in underneath us, but were gone by daylight. I also realized what I had risked by doing my impersonation of the Statue of Liberty in the middle of the jungle with a strobe light!"

During the late winter of 1970, 2nd Platoon and Delta Company stayed on the move. "We went from sleeping on hillsides, to skinny-dipping in a bomb crater in the flat lands, to fire bases big and little. We spent some time on FSB Mooney and FSB Rakkasan. I remember thinking at the time that Rakkasan was a fortress in the jungle and that we were untouchable until someone found a sandal in the wire and we knew we had been probed." Greek's occasional desire for living on the edge showed itself when the Chicago native volunteered to walk point. "I was too naive to be scared and no one really argued with me. It was uneventful that day except for something I'll always be grateful for. I was stopped at one point by our scout who was with us that day by a tug on my ruck. I had no idea why until he pulled me back and turned me enough to see the spider in the middle of the web I almost walked straight into. I swear that son of a bitch was as big as my hand. I sat down, had a smoke and was shaking for a good ten minutes."

Although the guidance of 2nd Platoon's boss, Lawrence Fletcher, would later come into question, especially his decisions around the first of May 1970, Avgerinos assessed his platoon leader highly. "The lieutenant seemed

2nd Platoon/Delta Company shortly before the 7 May battle at Fire Support Base
Maureen. Lt. Fletcher is fifth from the right, wearing a beret with the 101st emblem.
Courtesy Steve "Greek" Avgerinos.

to have a pretty good feel for the war. One night in particular I do remember. We had humped quite a ways one day and we were dragging ass. We were pissed because we were tired and wanted to set up for the night in a small valley, but he said no. We had found an abandoned bunker and an empty campsite earlier that day, and he told me he had a funny feeling about it. He picked a spot further ahead that was on high ground and that's where we were going. Thank God he did because that night they lobbed a half-dozen mortar rounds at us and not one came close. They did, however, hit where we would have been, had it not been for him." All in all the Greek felt that "we had a pretty good group in the 2nd Platoon."

One of Greg Phillips' first combat experiences in Vietnam involved setting up an ambush in an area where the Americans had cut back the thick vegetation using a device called a Rome plow. "Right in the middle of the second day, five North Vietnamese soldiers ventured into the Rome plow cut. They were looking for C-rations and things like that, which we GIs were always pretty careless about throwing away. No one ever ate the ham and eggs meal. Ham and eggs were always thrown away, so the outpost saw these guys come into the middle of the cut, called to the platoon that we had movement. So we all slipped over to that side, and here they are, five of them, out in the middle of a Rome plow cut like they're on a Sunday stroll. They never knew what hit them. We killed three of them, and, of course, everyone's shooting at them so you don't have a definite number of how many were there. One of the guys got away with a blood trail and we captured a fifteen- or sixteen-year-old kid."

At this time Phillips befriended a Vietnamese interpreter, a former enemy soldier who had come over to the American side as a so-called Kit Carson scout. "He took me under his wing, and I, in turn, took him under mine, and we had a lot of good times together. Once someone had received a *Playboy*, and he and I were looking at it, and there they had pictures of the moon landing. He looked—this is almost dusk, and he looked over at me and said, in essence, 'Explain what this is.' The moon was out, a big full moon—I pointed at the moon and said, 'GI on moon.' And he thought I had absolutely lost my mind. Thought I was kidding and laughed. He could not fathom that we had actually put people on the moon."

It was also during this time that Phillips witnessed the absurdity of the body count. This strategy of attrition, pushed by General William Westmoreland, called for commanders to achieve the crossover point at which more of the enemy were being killed than could be replaced. But in practice, the tactic led to many ludicrous claims. "One night," remembered Phillips, "we were about a klick, which I assume is about a mile, from one of the booby traps we'd set up, and we heard a huge boom, meaning the claymore [a particularly effective antipersonnel mine] had detonated. The next day we go in, and I didn't go into the base camp to check it out, but the other guys did and came back and said we killed a monkey. And then lo and behold we call the monkey in as a dead NVA. So I've often wondered when they say 'you killed one or two million North Vietnamese,' I wonder how many of them are really monkeys or roosters or chickens that we had submitted."

Gib Rossetter also recalled his baptism by fire and other earlier experiences with Delta Company. "Everything you heard was 'you guys are going to get killed first,' which ended up being the case in most instances. I remember when I saw that 'D Company,' I thought 'mortars should be E Company.' So I went into the hooch of the first sergeant of Delta Company and told them I thought there had been a mistake, that I was Eleven Charlie. He said, 'Are you Sergeant Gilbert Rossetter?' And I said, 'Yes, I am.' And he says, 'You're now Delta Company and this is an infantry company. Go down and get your M-16 and get your rations and get your ruck and get ready to go out in the field tomorrow morning.' So, then I got a little scared. Doing mortars was what I was trained for. I was really somewhat relieved then that I had taken that two-month survival course. The very next day, I was loaded on a chopper with four other guys, and met up with our company out in the field."

The Michigan man would never forget his first day of humping the boonies. "The CO was Captain Skinner, and he was a great guy. I remember him telling me, 'You'll be going to second platoon under Lt. Fletcher.' I was put in a squad [four men] along with another cherry. And him and I pretty much stuck together the first few day until others would warm up to us." It was during this early initiation period that Rossetter learned a harsh reality. "If a new guy would make it through the first couple of weeks and his first firefight, he had a pretty good chance. I saw many cherries, when a firefight would start, instead of ducking down real quick and locking and loading, they'd keep standing up looking around. Something about the new uniform and the new ruck sack made them pretty vulnerable over there." New members were also often shunned by battle-tested troopers. "They pretty much stayed away from the new guy. You felt pretty alone."

Rossetter was further shocked those first few days by the sheer difficulty of moving through jungles and mountains with all the equipment he was required to carry. "It seems to me that the very first day out there, we humped further and longer than I ever did the whole time I was in Vietnam. I remember getting so sore, so hot. Just wanting to stop and lay down and getting pushed from behind. 'Keep up, keep up' they'd say. I was dead tired. And I thought I was in great shape." Ruck sacks weighed anywhere from 100 to 110 pounds when cherries first started out. "Of course you carried—you had to carry at least four or five canteens, all the ammo I could put on, before I learned that you don't need to hump all that stuff. I could get my ruck sack down to about ninety pounds after I'd been there awhile, but that first day, first week, you had no idea. But I was so sore, I just wanted out of there."

Combat came to the soldier novice in a sudden and unexpected fashion. "My cherry was broke about two weeks after I first got out in the field. We were sent out on a reconnaissance to check out our perimeter and around our night position." After moving out seventy meters, "all of the sudden all hell broke loose. We were in an ambush, and I was one of those cherries that didn't drop down. A black guy, James Poe, grabbed me and pulled me down just as my helmet went flying off of me. I ended up wearing that helmet up until I lost it in July. It had a crease from where the AK round had hit my helmet. Anyway, I remember sitting there, laying there, just shaking." At first Rossetter found himself unable to react. "I couldn't fire that M-16. I could not get myself to take the safety off. Poe just kept yelling at me, 'Fire, Fire.' And after what seemed like ten minutes when realistically it was ten seconds or less, I took it off safety and just closed my eyes and started firing. A short time afterwards, after changing a clip, something hit me, a peace that I was okay, that I was going to be okay. And from that moment on, I was an infantryman. I'm sure that firefight didn't last more than thirty seconds." Intense combat thrusts a man into a unique and probably unwanted brotherhood. As Rossetter would note years later, at the moment of his first firing his weapon in actual combat, "my life changed forever."

Dick Doyle's recollections of his first encounters in southeast Asia also stand as vivid and disturbing. Typical of many who came to the war after 1969, Doyle found himself moved from group to group so that it was hard to develop a sense of unit tradition and, more importantly, camaraderie. Doyle, for example, served with three different units, which ended up being a negative factor. "One of the few positives that you have as an infantry soldier is that you have your buddies. When all is said and done, a soldier fights for his buddies and their preservation, not all the other bullshit you hear about. I was ripped away from my buddies not once, but twice, so by the time I was sent to 101st I had no trust nor desire to meet and have buddies." The Vermont man soon came to internalize his emotions, deciding "the only one that could be trusted for anything was me. In hindsight it cost me, as some of the small number of people I've remembered that I served with have formed strong bonds with others, and I have so little of that. They have stories of comradeship, and they can recall events where so and so did something, and I can't, because I was so ferociously internalized in my feelings and my window on events. I was very bitter about it all the time it happened and felt it was just part of the pattern of manipulation and destiny that seemed to be shaping up at the time." It would be Doyle's first experiences of witnessing an American killed in action that would stay with him the most profoundly.

"One day, in January 1970, while we were moving on patrol, our flank security spotted what appeared to be a vacated bunker. Immediately several guys took off to investigate with the platoon leader and the radio operator, David Farr, and we were ordered to pull off trail and stand fast. A bit of time went by, then the sound of an explosion. I knew it was in the direction of the bunker they were checking out, so I radioed Farr to get a sitrep, no reply." Doyle and a few others took off in a run toward the site of the explosion. "I was really upset that Farr was so incompetent that he wouldn't respond. When we got to the bunker there had been an explosion, a booby trap had been planted in the steps, which the lead guy had triggered by walking down into the bunker. I recognized Farr lying face down at the top and outside the bunker. The platoon leader was moaning and in a great deal of pain near Farr." Together, a medic and Doyle flipped Farr over. "The look on his face told me what I feared, that he was dead—slackness in his face, eyes empty, covered with dirt. Over the years the look on his face has blurred, but it was death. It was the first dead American soldier that I had seen. It rattled me to my core. Farr's job as RTO to the platoon

Kenneth David, "Little David," on the right and Gary "Oatmeal" Madden on the left. David's courageous actions on 7 May were a key element in fighting off the vastly superior number of NVA. For his actions, David received the Distinguished Service Cross, second only to the Medal of Honor. Courtesy Steve "Greek" Avgerinos.

leader had been my job less than two weeks before. I still see his lifeless face today when conditions trigger it. The thing that struck me was once the medic saw that he was dead, he instantly turned his attention to two other soldiers. There was no grieving, no emotion—nothing." When the medivac arrived it appeared to have a wounded VC on it. "We loaded the wounded, but they wouldn't allow us to load Farr on and we thought it was because the helicopter was too full due to the VC prisoner. We started yelling and screaming to pull his ass off the chopper. I felt a rage that I had never encountered in my entire life."

In a March 1970 letter, Ken David asked his father to send him a knife, one with "a ten inch blade and a case so I could wear it in my belt." David apparently sensed the coming storm. By mid-April, the time Ken Kays came to the field, all hell would break loose for the 101st and especially for members of Delta Company, 2nd Platoon.

7

They Stood Alone

Without doubt there were many difficult places and environments where U.S. troops endured combat in Vietnam. One might easily argue, however, that the arena where the 101st Airborne fought from 1968 to 1971 was one of the most hostile and difficult. Given the added political circumstances the 101st faced after 1969, fighting there verged on the unbearable. The dreaded A Shau Valley loomed as the dominant feature of this area of conflict. The valley, and the surrounding mountainous region, lay isolated in the northwest corner of South Vietnam and offered sanctuary for the North Vietnamese forces. Mostly absent of roads, far removed from major American bases, and possessing steep-sided, jungle-covered mountains, its close proximity to neutral Laos made the area an almost flawless haven for North Vietnamese troops hoping to stage operations in the low country to the east. The climate of this intimidating land further added to the woe of American GIs. Fog and heavy rain often socked in the mountain bases where the 101st units were typically located. Temperatures were volatile there as well—reaching over 100 degrees at times, not counting the dreadful humidity. But the fickle weather could change drastically from brutally hot to blustery cold, as 101st soldier Dick Doyle experienced. "We ran into some of the wettest and coldest weather I remember during my tour. Once we had two to three days of non-stop rain and wind with substantial drops in temperature. We were freezing and had no extra clothing available." Mike Bookser, another 101st trooper, wrote home in January of 1970 grumbling of the difficult weather conditions. "I'm still on Fire Base Rakkasan, but we've been socked in for a week. We were supposed to get off this hill on the 2nd, but after half the people got off helicopters, the clouds came in and stranded the rest of us. We've got to get out of here soon because rations are running low and ammo can't hold up forever." Despite all the discomforts, the scenery 101st members witnessed could be breathtaking, as described by Bookser in another letter. "I wish my whole tour in Nam would be like it is now. We're out in the woods and the birds are chirping and the stream is gently flowing by, the sun is bright and all is well. This place is just like you see in 'Tarzan' movies. Tonight I'm sleeping by a tree that is about twelve feet wide at the base. The vines around here are as big as a small tree, they even have bark on them."

Regardless of the pros and cons for the 101st soldier, the ever-growing presence of the North Vietnamese regular army (NVA) remained the most important and deadly feature of this rugged area. In order to deny the territory to the enemy for future excursions, the 101st Airborne Division had pushed into the rugged A Shau Valley area in March of 1969. By May of that year, the 101st discovered the enemy had heavily fortified themselves in places such as Hill 937, soon to become known as Hamburger Hill, where the NVA stood and fought for more than a hellish week before melting away into nearby Laos. While it was a military victory—more NVA were killed than Americans, and the NVA withdrew—by mid-1969, Americans back home had grown tired of "the body bags and the grimacing, ruin-lashed wounded—for it appeared to represent courage without progress, sacrifice without meaning."[1] With a politically sensitive Nixon holding to his 1968 campaign promise of bringing American soldiers home and turning the war over to the South, a new strategy emerged for the 101st Airborne. Withdrawing directly out of the A Shau Valley, the Screaming Eagles "drew back to a line of fire bases that could be reached by road in the foothills between the coast and the mountains as the northern monsoon began in mid-October of 1969."[2] A major 101st offensive would be carried out in 1970, once the monsoon waned. Over time, several of these mini-fortresses ended up being carved out on distant lonely mountaintops, accessible only by helicopter. They were given a variety of names: Jack, Rakkasan, Gladiator, and Maureen, among others. The fire base concept had been introduced early in the war and existed at that time as little more than temporary artillery emplacements established to support infantry operations in a given area. But after the NVA and Viet Cong cut back operations following the 1968 Tet offensive, U.S. military leadership began developing more elaborate bases as a way to draw the enemy into firepower traps. Fire bases now became semi-permanent fortresses, with dug-in gun pits, bunkers, and sandbags.

By 1969–70, the western area of Thau Thien province contained more than two dozen such bases scattered throughout the region, and they became a regular part of the common 101st soldier's life. Mike Bookser, with Bravo Company, vividly recalled life in one fire base, FSB Rakkasan, in late December of 1969. "We slept in bunkers while on Rakkasan. Bunker walls were made of sandbags stacked up to about five feet high with a 1/2 round piece of culvert pipe, or PSP [protective steel plating] placed on the sandbags for a roof. The culvert pipe would then be covered with sand bags. Since there were no windows in the bunkers, and we didn't have electricity, we made smudge pots out of ammo cans. We would fill the ammo can with dirt and soak the dirt with fuel oil. A match or cigarette lighter would be used to light the fumes of the fuel oil. There wasn't much light given off by the smudge pots and they did give off a black smoke but it was better than nothing."

It was hoped these bases, with their artillery firepower and abundant supplies for outgoing 101st troops moving out on search-and-destroy missions, would keep the enemy off balance, if not drive them completely out of the area. Ideally, this action would also allow the South to train and prepare for taking over the war, as well as allow for other American units to stand down. The 101st would guard the door while other American troops disengaged from the war. It was an unenviable and ultimately heartbreaking task. Unknown to 101st leadership, the North had been fortifying the area themselves, building complex bunker systems under the very noses of the Americans. As explained in a letter written by Mike Bookser to his future wife, the stealthy enemy lurked everywhere. "I was dropped off on FSB Jack and introduced to Captain Sullivan, the company commander for B Company. He pointed to a brown area in the valley where we were for the past four days and said that brown area is in the middle of the 9th North Vietnamese Sapper Regiment who were underground in tunnels. That made me feel real good." In another letter Bookser lamented to his future wife, "The VC and NVA dig underground tunnels so they can operate in an area that we have control. Bunkers are reinforcements that will stand up to bullets, mortars, artillery, and maybe even bombs if they are strong enough."

By April of 1970, enemy forces facing the 101st reached a greater level than during the brutal Tet offensive. Into this dangerous arena came Ken Kays and other Delta Company members. The company belonged to the 101st's 506th Regiment. Formed in 1942 as a parachute unit, the regiment had secured more than its share of glory in World War II. The unit took the motto "Currahee," a Cherokee word meaning "stand alone." By late winter of 1970, signs began to point to an oncoming clash for the Currahee and an opportunity to achieve more glory. The glory, however, would come at an immense price. Ken David's letter home suggested something was up by mid-March. Taken together, his correspondence offers insightful foreshadowing of the 7 May struggle.

On 14 March 1970, David wrote his parents, telling them "I didn't get much sleep last night because we were on 100% alert. For the first time I was really scared. To be honest everyone was." A week later David related, "The place is crawling with V.C. It will just be some time before we run into them." Finally, Ken David confessed to his family the details of what was now occurring in the 101st's area of operation. "I don't like to tell you things like this. That way you won't worry so much. Last night the firebase was hit. Since I've been here this is about the first time that it really seems like a war zone, and people are dying. Don't worry, I can take care of myself. Just say a couple of prayers for me in church, and don't worry, God is looking out for me."

Of obvious distress to his parents, a letter written after March contained even more detailed descriptions of combat. One dated the first of April told of a mortar attack. In the letter David grieves, "I don't want to be here, but I was told to go, so what can I say? How are you and everyone else taking it? Not too badly I hope. Don't worry I will take care of myself. I know how. Just think I have been here two months already. Only ten to go. It seems like forever, but really the time goes fast." A week later the young man reported, "We had a little misfortune to one of our platoons. It was nothing but one hell of a nightmare. At first there were all kind of explosions, and we believed that my platoon was being hit, but it was the other platoon, only 300 feet from us. The explosions lasted for about five to ten minutes, but it seemed like five months." (This was the attack in which Paul Frink died.)

By late April the increase in action moved Ken David to question the war. "Every time I think about it, I wonder why I am here." Also in late April, 2nd Platoon experienced its heaviest fighting to date. David did not wish to upset his parents or his girlfriend, but his need to share what he experienced superseded that concern. It must have been a terrifying read for his family. "I wasn't going to tell you or Annie, but I guess I should let you know. Before I do, I want you to know I am ok and in A-1 condition, and you don't have to worry. Well, last night my platoon got hit. It was about 1 am. We were out in the bush. We had our perimeter set up with me in the center with the Lt. I was lying on my right side sleeping when all of a sudden 'boom.' The sky lit up. We started to take satchel charges. They were landing all around us. Some came within five feet of me. I didn't get wounded—I'm fine." The satchel charges Ken David wrote of were typically canvas packs containing explosives that were dropped or thrown, a weapon the enemy used with chilling effectiveness. The scariest aspect of such an attack was that their use meant the enemy was at close hand.

Fire bases were now the focus of many attacks. Mike Bookser wrote home in mid-March telling of the grim scenes he witnessed just after an enemy attack on FSB Granite. "I was one of the first, if not first, slicks [helicopters] in to Granite for support that day, after they repelled the opposing force. When I got there, there were NVA draped over the artillery pieces that had been turned and were pointed at FSB Rakkasan. Several other NVA were laying on the ground. There were NVA bodies all over the place." On 25 April 1970, Bookser's company air assaulted by helicopter into FSB Maureen, an abandoned base the 101st was considering reopening. This occurred just days before Delta Company, along with 2nd Platoon, Ken Kays' future outfit, came to Maureen. Bookser recalled being unable to shake his sense that the area literally crawled with the enemy. "The area had beautiful lush green vegetation growing on the ridge line outside of the vegetation-less Maureen. As we got into the canopy the ground vegetation became less dense. We had moved approximately 300 meters from FSB Maureen when we made our first contact with the NVA at about 10:00 A.M. What we didn't know was that we were on top of an NVA stronghold dug underground."

What happened next for Bookser and his Bravo Company would foreshadow the plight of Delta's 2nd Platoon just days later. "I had begun the day thinking that it would be a fairly uneventful day. After all, we were going into a place we had watched B-52s bomb the week before. The mountain exploded for about half an hour. I thought for sure that nothing was left except a mopping-up operation. Boy was I wrong." As 25 April wore on, the fighting greatly escalated. Bravo Company discovered they were facing a large, well-entrenched, and determined enemy. Of great concern to Bravo Company, and later Delta, was the growing attrition rate the company experienced due to death, woundings, or other factors. Bookser recalled the problem: "The day we went to Maureen my squad totaled six, including me, and that wasn't unusual. Field strength was supposed to be fourteen. I had one guy out because his arm had been torn open by a centipede and another because he drank water out of a banana tree and broke out in blisters."

Eventually that day on Maureen, Bookser's platoon found its individual squads separated and pinned down. Bookser, himself a squad leader, sized up the situation and came up with a plan which would allow the platoon to better advance on the NVA. It called for his squad to move toward the enemy's perimeter. Realizing the great risk involved and that most of the other men in his group were either "short" or married, Bookser simply said, "Follow me if you want to." Everybody followed. Bookser would receive a severe wound that day, and later a Bronze Star with "V" device for his brave actions. Bookser's platoon sergeant, Jesse Issac, received a Distinguished Service Cross for his heroism on the same day. His company, thanks in part to Bookser's and his squad's performance, was able to disengage from the enemy. The "success" however, came at a steep price. "As I was crawling back to the rear, I saw two guys carrying a body. I asked who it was and they told me B. J. They stopped and laid the body down beside me. I looked at his face and began to cry." Bookser would spend several moments in tears before he moved on to the company's command post.

By this point in the war, more and more medics, like Ken Kays, came as conscientious objectors. During early April, Mike Bookser ran across one such medic. His deep religious convictions greatly impressed the tough-minded sergeant. "He told me that he didn't believe that men were supposed to kill other men and that's why he was a conscientious objector. I told him that I could understand his point, and it was not a problem with me, after all, medics were not in the field to fight they were in the field to patch up everyone else. This medic was shot four different times on April 25th while exposing himself to fire while rendering aid during the battle." John Smith also recalled another CO medic who served with the 101st during this time. Smith's platoon was preparing to move off a fire base into the jungle when "this little quiet guy, Bob Hayes, walked up to me and said something like, 'Sir, they told me to go with you. I am your medic.' We introduced ourselves and I instantly realized that this little guy was very different. He smiled, but even his smile was serious. He seemed oblivious to his surroundings. I instinctively knew he was a CO, and just as instinctively I knew he was for real. I met several COs who were philosophically opposed to war, but this guy, I just knew, was opposed to killing, period. Those other guys usually had some aggressive tendencies, and I just know that most of them would have picked up a weapon if they got boxed into a nice tight corner. Bob would have simply stood there and died rather than harm anyone, and I knew it the minute I met him. He was real."

Steve Gunn, another conscientious objector medic, also came to the 101st during the time of Ken Kays' service there. His letters home to his parents in Mississippi lend important insight into the daily life of a 101st medic in 1970. In early February of that year, when contact with the enemy remained light, Gunn wrote of his company's routine: "I've now been out in the field for six days. The last two days I spent with a couple of platoons from our company at an artillery base, and yesterday I came to the 2nd platoon. I think this is a relatively permanent place for me, although I may get switched to another platoon. This platoon moves around, changing positions everyday. They move to a dry position and hang around doing nothing, then send out one or two squads at night to set up an ambush. They either stay out all night or come back to the central position some time during the night." Gunn also reported to his parents about the supplies he carried as a medic, the same items Kays would have had to lug through the dense jungles. "I carry a lot of different things in my aid bag and sick call bag, though in small quantities. I have a large aid bag for wounds with 47 battle dressings, five IV bottles, a couple of inflatable splints and some gauze pads. My sick call bag is a lot smaller—about the size of a purse. I carry merthiolate, tape, gauze pads, a couple of creams for ringworm and rashes, pills for diarrhea and nausea and several types of antibiotics. I feel relatively well prepared for whatever may come up. If I can't handle everyday sickness, they probably need to be sent to the rear anyway."

By late March, Gunn's letters, like Ken David's, indicated an increase in enemy activity. Gunn's main distress, however, concerned a new company commander. By this time in the war soldiers typically dreaded any leader who was "gung-ho." Such a type could more easily get his men killed or wounded in a war from which everyone knew the U.S. was disengaging. "I'm out in the boonies again, i.e. off the firebase and humping around everyday. We left there a few days ago. We have a new commanding officer who is a gung-ho bastard, always killing gooks. He has been running us a little harder than the last commanding officer, moving more often and longer distances. He's a real-lifer type. He carries a shot gun and a belt full of shells, rather than an M-16, some sort of masculine symbol, I guess."

Kenneth Kays came to Vietnam in mid-April of 1970. The young Fairfield, Illinois, man later told a neighbor, Jon Simpson, that he was inappropriately placed in the field the very day of his arrival. Kays believed his lack of acclimation time was because of his conscientious objector status and because he had gone AWOL during his last leave home. It might also have been because by mid-April, with the sudden increase in fighting, medics were now desperately needed. At any rate, Kays experienced combat the first night he was there. The CO medic later told his neighbor the platoon leader had purposely sent him outside the perimeter into a great area of danger after the struggle had ended "because of my past." This past included Kays' resistance to army protocol throughout his training and his outspoken dislike of the war while in the states and as soon as he arrived in Nam. It did not help Kays' mood when he heard there was "a $1500 bounty for an army medic bag the enemy could bring in." Kays apparently felt like a marked man in terms of both the enemy and 101st leadership.

In fairness to his superiors, Kays had never been one to get along well with assertive authority. In a newspaper interview several months after the battle at Fire Support Base Maureen, Kays told a reporter, "They put me in the field early. I didn't really think I was ready to take care of wounded men. But we were hit almost every night in the field, so I learned quickly."[3] Whatever the situation, Kays was destined to experience a lonely sojourn in Vietnam. Platoon members did not usually draw near to cherries.

Kenneth Kays' reaction to his first combat experience is ironic given his later heroic response at FSB Maureen. A fellow medic, Ralph Matkin, remembered a brief and dramatic enemy encounter he and Kays endured while going out to help some local villages in a "safe" area during that first week Kays was in Vietnam. "Kays was the most recent 'FNG' at the battalion aid station at the time, and I have to admit, his counterculture rants were a pain in the ass and put most of us off at the time, which was pretty hard to do considering that 99.9 percent of us thought the war and the army sucked!" Matkin and the others grew particularly tired of hearing Kays tell of Woodstock and all the peace and love talk. Matkin assumed it was Kays' bad attitude that led to his being reassigned to the 506th Regiment and direct combat early in his tour. But it was Kays' reaction to a combat situation that most caught Matkin's attention.

> We were in a two-jeep "convoy" escorting a new physician to Phu Bai after completing a "medcap" mission to some local villages between Camp Evans and Hue. Our convoy came under attack on Highway 1, resulting in two American KIAs and two WIAs of its six members. I was in the trailing jeep with Ken. The lead jeep was hit with an RPG, killing the driver and rear passenger instantly and critically wounding the physician riding shotgun. My jeep veered to the roadside ditch and as much cover as it could afford. Its driver and I returned suppressing fire, but Ken would have no part of it and refused to take my weapon (M-16) when I scampered to the demolished lead jeep to check for survivors. As far as I (and my jeep's driver) could tell, Ken spent the entire time huddled in the ditch until we were rescued by a gunship and a truckload of reinforcements. He told me at the time, "I'm not going to get myself killed or kill anybody." Eventually I was wounded again at FSB Granite in late March 1970 during a coordinated NVA assault designed to overrun that position. It was another minor wound, but sufficient enough I suppose to get me sent to Zama Army Hospital in Japan. Two months later, I was reassigned to the States, spending my last fifty-three weeks on active duty as an emergency room tech at Tuttle Army Hospital in Savannah, Georgia. It was during the summer (1970) that I read about Ken's subsequent heroics at FSB Maureen.

Kays came to 2nd Platoon on 5 May 1970, when Delta Company landed by air on an abandoned fire support base with the harmless-sounding name of Maureen. It was not a good time for the platoon or Delta. Gib Rossetter remembered, "We seemed to be a kind of hard-luck company. In that first three months that I was there, we lost a few guys to our own artillery. We saw a lot of contact. It just seemed wherever we went, we'd find trouble." To make matters worse, at this point in the war many new men were coming into the 101st from other divisions, watering down the camaraderie. "In the first part of April we must have gotten anywhere from twelve to fifteen new guys in our company. I think they came mostly from the Big Red One and the 25th Infantry. Colors went home and of course the colors go home, but the soldiers stayed." One of the new people would become Rossetter's closest comrade. "Dean Finch and I instantly became best friends, and we both saved each other's lives throughout the rest of the year a few times. Wherever Dean was, Gib was; wherever Gib was, Dean was. I even talked him into carrying my radio for me for awhile. He was one of the best soldiers that D Company ever had."

In mid-March, Rossetter recalled things heating up. Aware that the war was for all purposes over, even the tough 101st sometimes had trouble getting men to fight. "We were going up this hill that intelligence told us was heavily bunkered, and we were to take it. Most of us in the company decided that we weren't going to do it. Captain Skinner, our commanding officer, was pretty furious with the company and ordered us to do it. I remember a major came out, threatening court martial. We ended up taking the hill, and we did get into heavy contact." This reversal of fortune boosted morale. "We got back into our base camp, Camp Evans, and we spent two or three days back there partying and eating steaks. That's when we rebuilt our little club back there."

In early March, while waiting to be reassigned, Greg Phillips met Dick Doyle. Their division was standing down but many of its members were being sent to other divisions instead of going home. Although from different parts of the country, the two young men instantly hit it off, and two weeks later the two came to Delta Company, 506th. Phillips remembered, "We were taken by helicopter to Company D in the field sometime toward the middle of March. I'm not exactly certain, I just know that it was toward the end of the monsoon season. I remember getting there right at dusk. We were introduced to Lieutenant Fletcher, to Greek, to Ken David, and some of the other guys. It was raining a little bit, and I was able to sleep just about all night." Phillips and his new mates soon tasted combat. "Toward the first of April, we were in night defensive position and about midnight, the North Vietnamese, I assume it was sappers, hit one of the platoons that had the commander of the company with them. They rained about twenty satchel charges on this group. The 2nd probably was within thirty-five to forty yards from them, and I can clearly remember how devastating it sounded." Most horrifying to the Alabama native was the severe wounding of two of the company's men. "Several of us went down the hill with strobe lights, weapons at the ready, and sat down in the valley for probably two hours or more waiting on that helicopter to come in and pick up the two wounded. It took them a couple hours to come up and get those two boys. The RTO for the captain died as a result of shock. I'll never forget the sight of a limb that's just barely hanging on to the other part of the leg."

Two days later, 2nd Platoon found itself in another night defensive position and coming under fire again. Phillips remembered, "They didn't get close enough to really hurt us. I know that I've got a piece of shrapnel in my eye and several other guys had wounds and so we were medivacked back to our base camp to check into the infirmary. I never will forget how the seven or eight of us were sitting in there, we've got various wounds and I said, 'Gee, something in here really stinks.' And lo and behold it was us. We just didn't realize how bad we smelled until we got into that sterile environment."

Alabama native Greg Phillips. Phillips left the relative safety of his foxhole to help defend 2nd Platoon's fragile perimeter on 7 May 1970. For his brave actions, Phillips received the Silver Star. Courtesy Greg Phillips.

Dick Doyle's first night in the boonies with D Company was also memorable. The Vermont man found himself shocked by his new squad leader's lack of time in the field and by some of 2nd Platoon's practices. "My squad leader came around and told me I had third watch; I think there were six or seven of us, so less than two hours. Next thing I know it's morning and I have never been awoken for watch. I went to my squad leader, and he kind of gave me this look and said they almost always assigned so and so to second watch because he fell asleep and everybody got to sleep all night. I don't suppose I have to elaborate about how crazy and irresponsible and dangerous that sort of mindset was." Doyle quickly attempted to address what he believed was a major problem. "Here I am the new guy and I felt my death warrant had just been signed. I asked to see the platoon leader, who was Lt. Fletcher, and he made some excuses how people were tired and they'd been working too hard, and he'd speak to the squad leader. I felt like I was now between the proverbial rock and hard place. I'd just ratted out my superior in my chain of command and gotten only a lukewarm response from his superior. I found out they had just fairly recently come into the mountains from patrolling the lowlands where nothing had happened, so their 'guard' was way down. All that was going to change." But Doyle remembered, "The squad shaped up about keeping better watch after that as far as I could tell, except they had snorers in the squad."

At this time 101st fighters knew they were involved in a seemingly useless war. Still, for the most part, they fought grimly on. Doyle recalled, for example, how a "sister platoon got whacked by NVA, small arms fire, but primarily satchel charges. We could hear the fight, as our NDP's were very close together, ours a little farther up a hill. All of a sudden we got the order to saddle up to go and relieve them. This was insanity of course, packing up your shit in the dark and moving out. As I came into perimeter, the medic was working on a wounded soldier; something in my memory tells me it was an officer, but I can't be sure. He literally had most of his ass blown off and appeared to be in shock, moaning, the bandages soaked through with blood. Certainly not good for our morale, but at least we felt like we were helping." The next morning Doyle found the company "sour, people tried to nap, too many people in too small an area, leaders looking disorganized." At this juncture Doyle had developed another beef with Delta Company procedure. "The enemy knew exactly where our sister platoon was because it had rained earlier in the night, so GIs put up ponchos to keep themselves dry and later the rain stopped and a partial moon rose so you can imagine nice wet slick ponchos as a giveaway target. The poncho thing was just another in the string of stupidity inflicted upon others and me. When I was with the 1st Infantry they would not issue grunts ponchos, just poncho liners, which were non-reflective and silent. 1st Infantry philosophy is it better to be wet than dead, which I agreed with."

As Doyle's and other members' recollections indicated, 2nd Platoon, now filled with young draftees and ninety-day wonders, was certainly not perfect. Larry McElroy, who came to the platoon for a day just before 7 May, recalled, "I had gone to sniper school, and when I returned to the field, my platoon was in contact so I was dropped with 2nd for a short while. Fletcher was nineteen, I think; too young probably to be a lieutenant [Fletcher was actually twenty-one]. Some members burned mail after sundown and two squads were very noisy after dark. They had no sound or light discipline. They scared the hell out of me that one night." McElroy, however, did not lay fault on anyone in 2nd Platoon for what occurred on 7 May. "The NVA knew every position on that hill."

Looking closely at the makeup of 2nd Platoon, one is struck by their youth, typical for the post-1969 period. Almost all were draftees. Likely the platoon was no better or worse than any other, just a group of young American men caught in a war many no longer understood, but who still attempted to do the right thing. Regardless, fate would soon dictate that they would experience one of the more bitter and intense firefights of the war. By early May of 1970, 2nd Platoon had been whittled down to some twenty men, down from the thirty or so men platoons ideally carried. Twenty-one-year-old Lt. Lawrence Fletcher, an OCS (officer candidate school) graduate, commanded the platoon. Platoon sergeant Steve "Greek" Avgerinos recalled that the small but feisty Fletcher came from the mountains of Virginia, and, after a moonshine conviction, had been given the choice of jail or army service. An intelligent man, Fletcher had opted for

Mike Bookser, right, with "Greek" Avgerinos. Bookser's Bravo Company air assaulted Fire Support Base Maureen just a few days before Kays' 2nd Platoon/Delta Company. Courtesy Mike Bookser.

officer candidate school. Greek's nickname for the plucky lieutenant was "underdog." Both Greek and 2nd's radioman, Ken David, thought their platoon leader was part Native American because of his dark skin. David remembered the lieutenant "did not shave much and had little facial hair." Photos of Fletcher show a dark, almost oriental-looking man of great intensity. The lieutenant, Ken David further recalled, "always had a 'Kool' clasped between his teeth and carried a canteen at his belt rather than the two the rest of his men carried." Unlike some platoon leaders, Fletcher was sharp enough to go to his sergeant, Greek Avgerinos, when he was unsure of what to do in difficult situations.

Greek himself had the reputation of being quiet but confident—a man you could depend on in combat. The tough Chicago native could also be generous, as Mike Bookser reported in a letter to his future wife. Bookser and Avgerinos had met briefly at FSB Rakkasan in late 1969. "Greek Avgerinos, the guy I went through NCO school with, gave me a Christmas present today," Bookser explained. "He had two cans of milk he got back in the rear, and he gave me one and said 'Merry Christmas.' It may not seem like much to you, but we were the only two guys with milk on the base." The small but thoughtful gesture at so difficult a time would stay with Bookser for the rest of his life.

In mid-April, baby-faced Ken David became Fletcher's radioman. At first David grew distraught when the lieutenant stayed so emotionally distant. "Later he told me that he had become good friends with the guy I replaced, and when that guy died it really hurt him. He didn't want that to happen again." Greg Phillips had his own perspective on the platoon leader. "We all had different opinions on Lt. Fletcher. I think he was a decent guy who tried really hard to do the right thing, but I also felt that he tried to get a little too close to the men. In management of any group of people, that isn't the thing to do. You have to stay above and apart to be a really good leader." Perhaps the biggest problem for the novice platoon leader was that "Fletcher was not in favor with Captain Workman, the company commander, from my viewpoint. Fletcher was an OCS guy and Workman a West Point man." In one instance, Phillips recalled, "Fletcher was firing a M-72 LAW into the jungle, trying to hit an enemy mortar placement. He really didn't know where it was, just firing into the jungle. Workman got on to the lieutenant because he didn't clear the area behind him."

The rest of the platoon hailed from all over the country and had many personality types. Dark-haired Greg Phillips was one of the larger young men in the platoon, standing six feet tall and weighing more than two hundred pounds. Reserved at first, Phillips grew outgoing and charming as he got to know a person better. Phillips could also be stubborn and determined, as the night of 7 May was to soon prove. Gib Rossetter, one of three Michigan men in the unit, was remembered by a later platoon leader as an NCO who got things done without being mouthy or tough. Lean and a couple of inches short of six feet, Rossetter "was willing to accept the position of platoon sergeant because he trusted himself more than he trusted anyone else at the time. He was quietly self-assured. Yet, he was just a kid leading kids." One of the favorites in the platoon was southeast Missouri native Dean Finch. John Smith thought Finch "more of a 'what you see is what you get' kind of guy. Not at all sophisticated, he had a country boy charm and good looks without being a hayseed. Despite a medium stature, he was robust, good and strong physically as well as mentally. He too was sort of quiet, at least not obnoxious, but he leaned toward the good-time side of life. He didn't have an easy smile; he had an easy laugh. If there was fun to be found, Dean was looking for it."

Another likeable soldier in the platoon was Peter Cook, a twenty-year-old from North Adams, Massachusetts. A friendly young man from the rural Berkshire region, where as an adolescent he had participated in 4-H, Cook, like so many of his 2nd Platoon comrades, had come to Vietnam via the draft. Dick Doyle drew especially close to Cook. Tall, lean, and dark-haired, "Peter was from Clarksburg, Massachusetts, the northwest part of state, hugging Vermont. We hit it off really well because I was from Vermont." The two men often shared a foxhole, and Doyle remembered

2nd Platoon best friends Dean Finch, left, and Gib Rossetter out in the field.
Courtesy Gib Rossetter.

how the young Massachusetts native "most often talked about his wife and family back home." In one instance, Doyle recalled he and Cook being next to another foxhole pair who were "throwing their grenades in a mad minute and this sending shrapnel whizzing by our heads. Come to find out, they were playing 'chicken' to see how long they could hold the grenade after pulling the pin."

Besides Gib Rossetter, there were two other Michigan natives in the unit—tall, broad-shouldered Gordon Scheerhorn and Thomas Schofield. John "Curt" Alexander, who spoke with a conspicuous drawl, hailed from the mountains of North Carolina, although he had spent several years living in Arizona. Robert Rosas, a tall, husky, no-nonsense Texan of Mexican descent, was remembered by John Smith for his frequent calmness under

2nd Platoon's John "Curt" Alexander on the left and "Greek" Avgerinos on the right, finding protection from the brutal Vietnam sun. Courtesy Steve "Greek" Avgerinos.

fire. "A cool guy, but not one to mess with. He was a good machine gunner; saving our asses at a hot LZ [landing zone] when three dinks came sauntering in like they were on a nature hike." John "Ernie" Banks' light hair and complexion made him especially vulnerable to the savage sun of Vietnam. Yet Gib Rossetter recalled that the tall skinny youth "was an excellent machine gunner and very good in a firefight."

Another machine gunner in the platoon was a twenty-two-year-old named Lloyd Jackson, a Native American from Nevada. Greg Phillips remembered Jackson as a good, dependable soldier. "When I arrived at Delta Company's night defensive position in the jungle in March of 1970, I had the chance to meet most of the guys during my first few days with the platoon. Other than Greek, David, Doyle, and Fletcher, the one person I

Hard-luck Lt. Lawrence Fletcher, 2nd Platoon's leader. Fletcher was the first casualty of the Fire Support Base Maureen firefight. Courtesy Steve "Greek" Averginos.

remember best is [Lloyd] J. J. Jackson. I'm not certain why he was called J. J., but I assume it was because he could have been a junior. J. J. was the machine gunner in our squad, and a better soldier I have never met. He was a fierce combatant." Phillips discovered Jackson could be wise as well as fearless. "Jackson told me that he believed he would have been in line for a squad leader position until I showed up. He felt that I had displaced him for that position due to the fact that I had more experience than he. When he told me this there wasn't one ounce of jealousy in his voice. Truth be known he was a much better soldier than I. He just hadn't been exposed to as much combat."

Jose Gonzalez, a twenty-year-old Mexican-American from California, humped ammo for Jackson. Jose was considered by his fellow comrades to be a quiet, pleasant young man who longed for the day he could go home to his close-knit family. Robert Lohenry, a twenty-one-year-old platoon member from Chicago, also came to Vietnam compliments of the draft.

Joseph Redmond, like Lohenry, came from Illinois and was a twenty-five-year-old "lifer." Greg Phillips recalled that Redmond "had just come in from Germany and appeared to be a career guy."

The platoon, typical of this juncture in the war, found itself understaffed in early May of 1970. Dick Doyle, Sam Moore, Elmer Jurgens, and James Poe were on medical leave. Anthony Aquiningoc was receiving dental treatment and Tim Runyard was on R&R. Less than a week before 2nd Platoon came to Maureen, Dick Doyle had written his friend Greg Phillips, razzing him about the comforts he now enjoyed while convalescing from a serious hand infection. The infection, Doyle would later reflect, "probably saved my life." In the letter to his friend, Doyle teased, "Beautiful Cam Rahn Bay! Sidewalks, PA's with liquor, air-conditioned winds, mess halls, everything, female nurses, flush toilets, hot water in sinks and showers, TV, movies at night, bookstores, Red Cross center, Mars stations, beds with 6" mattresses, sheets top and bottom, blankets, etc. It's really great here. Don't know how long I'll be here—forever I wish." On a darker note, the concerned Doyle penned, "Hope you guys stay on the firebase and away from the shit. Stay clear of the gooks." Ironically, Phillips would not receive the letter until he was recovering from his own wounds received in the 7 May battle. At any rate, Doyle's optimistic hope that his platoon would stay in a safe place would soon be brutally dashed.

Official documents indicate that on 5 May 1970, Delta Company now faced elements of the 803rd North Vietnam Army (NVA) Regiment, along with an elite sapper group.[4] The sappers were among the most highly trained and motivated troops in the entire NVA. Kurt Maag remembered hearing that "NVA sappers had a major base just south of Maureen." Whatever the exact situation, the enemy here clearly meant business. Their mastery of the area further enabled them to spot any vulnerable points, especially a situation where a lone platoon might become separated to some extent from its larger company. Such would be the fate of 2nd Platoon on late 6 and early 7 May 1970.

At the beginning of May, back in the world, student protests against the war reached a fever pitch with Nixon's invasion of Cambodia, followed shortly by the Kent State shootings on 4 May. In sympathy for those killed at Kent State, on 7 May, the day of Ken Kays' own hellish day in Vietnam, students at Southern Illinois University, where Kays had recently attended, literally shut the university down with the most violent riots in protest against the war in the school's history. Kays, however, remained totally unaware of these events. His college days now seemed distant—of another world. On 5 May, Delta Company, under the command of Capt. Donald Workman, air assaulted by helicopter onto an abandoned fire base marked on the map as FSB Maureen. Captain Workman, a hard-nosed West Point grad, was known to all by his call sign—Ranger.

Two events occurred at this time which greatly disturbed Greek Avgerinos. The first involved 2nd Platoon leader Lt. Lawrence Fletcher. "Before we went out to Maureen, Lieutenant Fletcher got a 'Dear John' letter. He and I talked, and he told me how bad he felt. I don't remember him quitting or being insubordinate in any way. He wasn't that kind of guy. He was just heartbroken and looked like a guy who had lost the will to live. I had never seen him like this. He was always our leader and a guy to whom I always looked up. The lieutenant told me that he had requested a transfer and that he wouldn't be going out with us. I told him I understood and that we'd be ok." The other occurrence involved the company's Kit Carson scouts, former enemy soldiers who had come over to the American side. "One thing that really struck me as odd was that when we got ready to go out to Maureen, the Kit Carson scouts who were usually with us were nowhere in sight. Someone said out loud what most of us were thinking: 'they know we are going into some heavy shit and they don't want any part of it.' We'll never know for sure, but looking back, it seemed that truer words were never spoken."

Ken David remembered a different version of why Fletcher did not initially go with 2nd Platoon. The Virginia native had apparently grown angry with higher command over an earlier incident and wrote President Nixon. "Fletcher wrote a letter to the president, but Nixon never received it. The rear retrieved the letter and sent out a special bird to get only the lieutenant. Fletcher went before a review committee and his punishment was to be payroll master for the month, and he could not leave the bush until the day his R&R started. May 7 was the first day of his R&R." Sometime during that first day of Delta's assault on the abandoned fire base, Fletcher returned to his unit. Greek Avgerinos later recalled the platoon leader "heard what was happening to his platoon and asked permission to join us. He told me that whatever else had happened, he belonged with us. He didn't have to be there, but I was glad as hell to see him."

Despite artillery supposedly prepping the landing zone earlier that day, Delta Company landed on a hot LZ. It was only when the assault was in progress that Greg Phillips realized "in typical army fashion, they had been prepping the wrong landing zone." The company landed mid-afternoon and "incurred heavy, heavy hostile fire from the enemy surrounding this mountaintop. I was told at that point in time that some of the GIs spied a red-headed advisor with the North Vietnamese regulars, which would lead me to believe that there was a Russian involved in the battle." The heavy fire from the enemy included .51-caliber machine guns and rocket-propelled grenades. One of the rocket-propelled grenades exploded in front of 2nd's medic. "He sustained a wound to his chest and was medivacked out," Greg Phillips remembered. The medic's replacement was short but muscular Ken Kays.

Dean Finch, Gib Rossetter's best buddy in 2nd Platoon, turned twenty-one the day Delta Company landed on Maureen, but he had little time to reflect on what is a pivotal birthday for most young people. Richard Drury, a Michigan native and member of another Delta platoon, recalled how people "just hated to fly into Maureen because it was so small." Drury's first combat experience was on 5 May, and the novice warrior found himself shocked at the sight of two headless enemy soldiers laying there when the company jumped from the helicopters. "Someone put 101st emblems on the bodies and threw them over the cliff." This act might explain the furious attack by the NVA on 2nd Platoon two days later.

Because of the heavy enemy fire, Delta was unable to leave the mountaintop on 5 May. The next morning Delta Company did move out, but in separate groups. Dale Tauer, a Minnesota native who served in another platoon, recalled that many members of the group, when leaving the landing zone, grew "upset because we were separated when we went off Maureen. This didn't make sense to a lot of the guys who had been in the field for awhile." Greg Phillips soon realized to his dismay that "the NVA were dug in all around the mountain. Four of us were on the line when we came off of the fire support base. There was a point man [Tom Schofield]. I, as a grenadier, was the slack man, meaning I walked second in line, and then there were two others. Anyway, we four were on a line going into this bunker complex when a North Vietnamese regular opened fire on us, and one of our guys got wounded in his arm and his rear end and was medivacked out." Surprisingly, the North Vietnamese got away from the Americans "because of the sheer shock and surprise. Then, even after we opened up, our fire was ineffective against them. They were just too well dug in. We moved further on through this bunker complex and then attempted to move up another mountaintop and once more encountered heavy resistance from the enemy. They had dug in at yet another set of bunker complexes and were firing .51-caliber machine guns." F-4 tactical air strikes were called for but proved "ineffective inasmuch as they continued to keep us pinned down as a company, and for the rest of the afternoon we were not able to move forward."

Radioman Ken David also remembered that grinding first day. "We left the base for a company assault with twenty-plus helicopters. They had artillery for hours prepping one area, and at the last minute they took us somewhere else. I was on the sixth or seventh bird when the VC opened up. When we leaped off, Fletcher popped red smoke—the LZ was hot. No more birds landed. Our medic got it going off the other side of the helicopter. Ken Kays came to replace him shortly. During this time Fletcher was running to a hole and bullets were hitting the ground behind him, causing the dust to fly. Later, a light rain hit us." Delta Company spirits had ebbed

Gib Rossetter at Camp Evans, about to leave on a mission. Courtesy Gib Rossetter.

especially low by this time. Ken David, for example, found himself "tired of all the firefights, not sleeping and not being able to cry, but I just keep pushing myself." Many talked "about re-upping to get out of the jungle."

As noted, it was then that Ken Kays came to 2nd Platoon. Gib Rosset-ter recalled, "Most of the medics that were in our company leading up to Ken were not conscientious objectors, and they'd carry rifles, so I certainly remember the first time seeing Ken and him not having an M-16 along. I thought he was kind of crazy, but then again medics were more for the wounded—for helping wounded more so than fighting. My personal view is that it took a lot of guts to go out into an infantry company, out in the field knowing that you're going to see contact, and not have a weapon. At the same time I respected Kays' views against a weapon." Curt Alexander also remembered the new medic because of his amazing upper-body physique. "He just looked like a solid block of muscle."

As the afternoon of 6 May grew long, three undermanned platoons of Delta Company moved to fix night defensive positions. Here the story becomes shrouded in the fog of combat. All previous accounts, such as Keith Nolan's excellent book *Ripcord: Screaming Eagles Under Siege, Vietnam 1970,* lay the blame for 2nd Platoon's catastrophe squarely at the feet of Lt. Lawrence Fletcher. Nolan asserted, "The three platoons moved off the hill in three different directions, the 2nd Platoon under 1st Lt. Lawrence E. Fletcher returning to Maureen to set up an NDP in the middle of the abandoned firebase after heavy contact with the NVA below the hilltop on May 5. Fletcher spent the next day, May 6, on patrol. Running out of daylight before a new night defensive position could be found, Fletcher opted to return to Maureen."[5] Other accounts of the battle report the same thing.[6] Returning to a previously occupied night position in heavily infested enemy country would have broken a cardinal rule of fighting.

Ken David, Fletcher's radioman, remembers a different scenario. "The company left the landing zone [6 May], and before dark Captain Workman ordered Fletcher to go back up to the top and secure it for the night. Fletcher tried to tell the captain we were down to only eighteen men and would be spread very thin up there, but we were ordered to go anyway." Greek Avgerinos also maintained his platoon leader had been ordered back to the original landing spot on Maureen. "We were losing daylight quick, and the lieutenant was told to set up on the hill." Greek, however, "thought it was the right thing to do because the high ground would be easier to defend; especially since we were not at full strength. I think we were down to eighteen or nineteen." In Greek's thinking, it would be the company's position down the ridge, and not 2nd's, that would be most apt to be attacked that night.

Gib Rossetter had a slightly different memory of how 2nd Platoon came to make an NDP on Maureen. "We stayed up there at night on 5 May as a company, and the next day we split up in three different directions in the area. I remember it was foggy and misty. 2nd Platoon came up onto a bunker complex and some tunnels. 3rd Platoon came over and a few guys went into the tunnels, but they did not find anything that I recollect. It was our platoon's job to secure that area. We stayed there most of the afternoon while 3rd Platoon continued on. Finally, it was getting somewhat dark, and the decision was made by Lt. Fletcher that we had to find a night position and find it pretty quick. He decided that we should go back up onto Maureen and stay there through the night because we had stayed by that bunker complex for so long that we didn't find any better, and there were foxholes up there. So we went back up onto Maureen and got into positions."

Whatever the circumstances, Fletcher and his men quickly set up a hasty defense. The primary problem was the lack of manpower. Nine two-man foxholes were placed around the perimeter of an area roughly a hundred yards long and fifty yards wide. The rest of Delta were dug in some distance south and down the slope from where 2nd hunkered in for a long night. The platoon's situation was precarious because, for some unknown reason, original squads were split up. Still, many in the platoon sensed no imminent danger. Steep-sided mountain slopes were at the edges of the positions, with the most difficult slopes being on the east side, where Greg Phillips set up for the night with foxhole-mate Thomas Schofield. "The mountaintop on that side had extremely steep cliffs. That was one of the reasons that I chose that side of the perimeter to set up my squad's point man [Tom Schofield] and me. We set out claymore mines and then prepared for a long night."

The steep sides at the east edge of the abandoned base gave others a false sense of safety as well. Gordon Scheerhorn recalled how "we were only on half alert, but I don't think we were carrying out even that. Everyone seemed to be asleep." Over on the west side, Curt Alexander felt safe enough to make a place to sleep outside his foxhole. Greg Phillips later concluded that many in the platoon on the west side likely slept outside their holes that night. "It was harder digging over there. The hole I later occupied with Ken David on that side barely held the two of us and was really shallow. Our side [east] had old bunkers with the top off so we were in a better position than the west side." But some of the men, like Gib Rossetter, still worried as the night rapidly set in. "The positions were quite a ways away from each other. It didn't feel right to me at the time. Bob Lohenry, my foxhole partner, and I didn't sleep at all that night."

As 2nd Platoon struggled to get some much-needed rest after a long, nerve-racking day of searching through enemy bunkers, their greatest fear would have been a satchel charge attack by sappers. Dick Doyle recalled seeing a satchel charge demonstration at Camp Evans before being sent out to join 2nd Platoon in March of 1970. Apparently, the 101st wanted its soldiers to come to respect this wicked weapon. "It was a square block of explosive material about two feet long and two feet wide and was wrapped with bamboo strips. They would attach a fuse length to determine how quickly it would blow and may have added some metal for a shrapnel effect. NVA used to routinely check out our NDP sites after we left and dig up our waste, including C ration cans, and use them as metal for their satchel charges. The size of charge could vary, depending upon desired explosion or blast—some were sophisticated and some were rudimentary." The typical tactic for using the satchel charge involved the sappers creeping "up on your position and being within arm tossing range, then finding a low spot or depression in the ground. The 'low spot' is very important as it puts them just under your small arms fire, so you are firing away like crazy but hitting nothing. Then they light their fuses and lob the satchel charges in on the troops. I'd say it takes nerves of steel to do this, but they had those. Usually they would have a few well-positioned and covered troops firing their small arms to create a diversion and draw fire away from those with satchel charges. One way to counter this is to lob grenades along with small arms fire and blow claymore mines."

Apparently the NVA thought 2nd Platoon especially vulnerable. The Americans lay relatively separated from the rest of Delta Company, which sat further south down the steep mountain. Further, due to 2nd's return to a previously occupied spot, the enemy now knew the location of every 101st trooper, including where Fletcher and his radioman, Ken David, rested. Finally, the enemy may have been motivated by an event two days earlier, when two dead NVA had been thrown off Maureen after having 101st patches placed on them. The NVA struck with a unit larger than company size, including elite sappers, as well as with the all-important element of surprise. North Vietnamese military records show the enemy had great faith that their elite sapper units would be able "to find enemy gaps and weaknesses . . . and launch attacks and ambushes," which would erode the Americans' strength. These attacks were to be fierce and unexpected to the extent that 101st troopers would find themselves unable to "eat or sleep."[7]

At the annual Ripcord reunion in July of 2005, five of the survivors of 7 May talked for some time about the location of the platoon that night. Out of this discussion came a rough and tentative map. As best as can be ascertained from these survivors' memories, Fletcher, his radioman Ken David, and platoon sergeant Greek Avgerinos had dug in at the nine o'clock position, on the west side of the perimeter. Curt Alexander and a forward observer named Brunson occupied the eight o'clock location. South, at roughly seven o'clock, rested J. J. Jackson and Jose Gonzalez, manning the important light machine gun. Gib Rossetter and Robert Lohenry were at the five o'clock position, at the southeast portion of the circle. Greg Phillips with Thomas Schofield and Gordon Scheerhorn with Robert Horton were dug in at different places along the steep east side. At one o'clock lay Rosas and Kenny Kays, the platoon's recently arrived medic. Dean Finch, "Ernie" Banks, and Richard Staat occupied the eleven o'clock spot, while Robert Berger, Peter Cook, and Joseph Redmond were just to the north of Fletcher's foxhole. In all, twenty-one men were now dangerously stretched over a large area, leaving dangerous gaps. Perhaps it was these gaps, along with the cover of darkness, which allowed the enemy to come undetected into the very midst of the Americans. They quickly went for the kill, going first after Fletcher and the radioman.

2nd Platoon's Peter Cook on the left, Dick Doyle on the right. Doyle carried a great amount of survivor's guilt after his friend Cook died at Fire Support Base Maureen and for having himself missed the battle. Courtesy Richard "Dick" Doyle.

Ken David later recalled that the enemy that night "came in wearing only black loincloths and cloth tourniquets around their arms and legs. They wore tourniquets in case they got injured, so they could stop the bleeding and keep fighting." The hardest hit sections were along the northwest, west, and southwest parts of the Americans' perimeter, where the mountain was less steep. Curt Alexander remembered how, at about four o'clock in the morning of 7 May, Jackson woke him as he slept on top of the ground next to his foxhole. "J. J. whispered, 'I've got little men out there,' and we started throwing grenades." Unknown to the Americans, sappers had already moved into position. All at once a satchel charge exploded at Alexander's feet. The thunderous blast blew off a leg and made bloody meat out of one of his hands. "The only thing I remember after that is someone, maybe an NVA, taking my weapon. I guess I must have looked dead." Dean Finch, who had dug in somewhere on the northwest part of the defense line, was up relieving himself in the dark around four o'clock when he thought he noticed two men standing nearby. The night was clear and moonless. Thinking one of the shadowy forms might be Bob Rosas, Finch asked the closest figure for identification. Rosas responded. Then Finch asked the other to identify himself. A burst of AK fire answered the query.

"It was just one loud long bang," Finch recalled, "just total chaos and our guys screaming for the medic. People were also howling that they [NVA] were in our perimeter." One sapper threw a satchel charge into Finch's hole. "I threw it out and got him with an M79." Finch moved quickly from his position to where he believed Fletcher was and found the platoon leader had already been killed and that the enemy was everywhere. Finch was sent back to defend his original position. Although he always carried a lot of extra ammo, three bandoliers with twenty-one clips each, Finch would go through his entire supply before the terrible night was over.

Just below and southeast of Ken David and Greek Avgerinos, Gib Rossetter found himself fighting for his life as shadowy figures, stripped down to black shorts, appeared and just as quickly melted back into the darkness. As they ran by Rossetter's and other GIs' positions, they hurled something that looked like sparklers. "Early in the morning, I don't know, maybe four o'clock, the first thing I heard was satchel charges going off inside our perimeter, and then all hell broke loose. We were taking enemy fire in front of us." More disturbing to Rossetter, however, AK rounds were soon going off inside the perimeter. Stunned, the Michigan native realized the enemy had broken their defenses. The vague forms seemed to be everywhere. "I was concentrating on firing in front of me, and checking behind me quite often as well. I could tell that the positions to my right and to my left were firing also. Then, after some time, I could tell that the position to my left [Jackson and Gonzalez] was not firing anymore." Concerned, Rossetter started yelling over to try to see what had happened to the men in the neighboring foxhole, where J. J. Jackson's machine gun could be essential for survival. Getting no response, Rossetter made a tough decision. "I told Bob Lohenry that I was going to go over to that other position to check them out. I remember Lohenry was pretty nervous. He didn't want me to leave him there." Rossetter found Jose Gonzalez dead. "Jackson was wounded really bad, and so I was calling for the medic and Ken Kays came leaping over and dragged the wounded soldier out." Kays found a spot toward the center of 2nd Platoon's defensive line to place the mangled Jackson. After carrying out essential aid, the young medic hurried back to the edge of the perimeter to look for more wounded.

At the heart of the platoon's command center, baby-faced Ken David had just finished his radio watch when "Fletcher sat up, and in a low voice said, 'What was that?' Then I heard grenades and M-16 fire towards Fletcher—a full magazine from what sounded like near our right front. The NVA had taken the position already." The radio sat between David and Greek. "As the satchel charges were being thrown in our position, I was calling for help over the radio and throwing back the charges. There were all kinds of explosions and noise." What happened next to "Little David" would later be difficult for the Ohio native to comprehend or share. "All of a sudden it was peaceful and quiet. I noticed that I was looking down from above. I was out of my own body. I saw myself lying still, Fletcher was still, and Greek had moved to the middle of our perimeter with the radio. I saw people running and flashes of light rifle fire. As I was floating further away, all I could say was that I have to get back to help them. Later at the hospital, Greek told me I was lifeless for some time." Suddenly David remembered being hurled back into the melee of explosions, rifle fire, and screams. "The next thing I remember I grabbed my helmet and put it on only to find out later it was on backwards. The NVA were all around me throwing satchel charges." David threw some back, others he ignored. Although the slight man with the backward helmet didn't look like a warrior, Greek Avgerinos's "Little David" was about to demonstrate a fury that would stun his attackers.

The stealth of the enemy also surprised battle-tested Steve Avgerinos. Greek, who lay close to Lt. Fletcher when the attack began, recalled, "Kenneth David had just finished his watch and told me he thought he heard movement. I told him I would keep my ears open, but that I thought it was just a case of nerves. The first satchel charge landed right next to the hole I was sitting in with the radio. It was instinct that made me scoop it up and out and it went off seconds later in midair in front of me. I lobbed two or three hand grenades out in front and couldn't tell you if I hit anything because it was pitch black a yard down. I turned to my right at the sound of small arms fire that hit Lt. Fletcher as he slept. He only lived long enough to call out 'Greek, help me,' but I couldn't get to him. I believe he died almost instantly." Fletcher's frightful plea would stay with the platoon sergeant the rest of his life.

At almost the same moment as Fletcher's death, Greek witnessed an explosion where John Banks' hole was and then saw a dark figure come bounding past his hole. "I think it may have been one of the sappers, but I couldn't be sure. There were additional explosions to my left, one of which I believe was in the hole where Curt Alexander was. I was able to get off about two magazines before my M-16 jammed completely. I didn't need to call Kenneth David for help because he was already there. He took over for a short period while I moved to the center of the perimeter with the radio. I looked to the opposite side of the hill for help because all the activity seemed to be concentrated on our side. It made sense that they were trying to knock out the radio as they always did." The fearless Avgerinos made an excellent target standing in the middle of the hill with no weapon and no cover. 2nd Platoon, those who could still fight, found it almost impossible to find a target, even when illumination was later dropped over their positions. The shadows would keep the Americans off balance, and they would hear a brief engagement on one side of the defenses, then on another. Gib

Rossetter recalled the agony of thinking he might have hit some of his own. Such were the multiple terrors of that night.

South of the struggle, the rest of Delta Company heard explosions and gunfire, then received a frantic radio call from Greek Avgerinos. Captain Workman immediately ordered a platoon to head north up the ridge to help the 2nd. On the way, however, the group was ambushed and stopped cold. It was simply too dark to proceed. Dale Tauer remembered what the beginning battle looked and sounded like from Delta's headquarters located down the mountain ridge. "It was early in the morning when one hell of a firefight started. First came the claps of exploding satchel charges. Then we heard a frantic voice on the radio calling in — 'enemy in our lines.' Everyone was thinking, 'my God the enemy has penetrated their perimeter.'" Now the rest of Delta could only wait and listen to the gruesome sounds of battle as 2nd Platoon fought alone for its life. Being young and human, Delta Company members listening to the fighting likely thanked God they were not a part of what was unfolding just a short distance away.

The pivotal part of the battle would soon be reached. Greek Avgerinos had pulled the command post back toward the center of the NDP where he could more safely call in air support. Of course, in this instance, safety was a relative term. Before Greek left the old position, he asked Ken David to try and hold this essential place on the west side. Realizing "Little David" needed more help or the perimeter would be lost, the platoon sergeant shouted for someone from the comparable safety of the east edge to come help. Only defiant Alabama native Greg Phillips answered the call. When Phillips arrived at the middle of the perimeter, where Greek labored to keep in contact with the outside, he was greeted by a satchel charge. "It went off probably within about ten or fifteen feet of me. I had no way of getting away from it. To this day I have problems with my hearing in my right ear, and it's getting progressively worse." But there was little time for pain. Avgerinos hurriedly told Phillips the platoon had been hit hard on the western flank and that the platoon leader was dead, along with many others killed or severely wounded. Phillips found it hard to believe that, as best Greek could tell, only diminutive Ken David remained holding that side of the perimeter. "David was really an extremely young guy and a rather timid fellow. He was put in a terrible position all by himself on that edge." Amazingly, Ken David had been single-handedly holding off the enemy but would probably not be able to for much longer. After consulting with Avgerinos, Phillips ran to the side of the perimeter, located David, and leaped into the foxhole with him. "That hole only covered half our bodies," Phillips recalled. To make matters worse, Phillips quickly realized that David was the only survivor, or at least the only one able to fight, at that essential section of the perimeter.

Just after Phillips arrived to assist Ken David, the battle seemed to intensify. Fortunately, Greek's radio efforts began to pay off. Greg Phillips remembered, "While we were engaging the enemy, we had numerous Cobra gunships come in to support us. Greek was also calling in artillery fire, trying to help us keep the enemy off." One thing David and Phillips had in their favor was the steepness of the slope the enemy had to navigate to get at the Americans. Phillips, however, chalked up his and Ken David's success to another element. "To this day, I feel that without Greek calling in the gunships and the artillery, that they would have easily overran us, because there were only two of us there. And had the NVA gotten past us, they probably would have wiped out the rest of the platoon at that point in time."

The two men quickly set off trip flares four or so feet in front of their shallow foxhole so Cobra helicopters could run their miniguns right up to the edge of the Americans' position. Still, the enemy stubbornly pushed on at the two 101st troopers. Phillips recalled seeing a satchel charge tumbling through the air. "It hit roughly two feet in front of me. I had really nowhere to go, but lay there, and fortunately, this satchel charge was a dud." The battle now became a face-to-face encounter. An enemy soldier suddenly appeared down the slope, aiming a rocket-propelled grenade at the two Americans. The projectile "literally hit on the back side of our placement and exploded," remembered Phillips. "I got hit in the left rear part of my head with four pieces of shrapnel. Kenneth David got it in his lower back and also sustained eardrum damage. We both reacted, I guess as anyone would, and shouted in pain as the hot shrapnel hit us."

A grenadier, Phillips had a grenade launcher lying on the edge of the foxhole. It was about to come in handy. "After shouting in pain from the shrapnel, I looked up and saw, probably fifteen or twenty feet in front of me, a North Vietnamese regular with an AK-47 opening fire on me. These AK-47s are extremely hard to shoot, and being small people as the North Vietnamese were, most of the time when they opened fire with one, they didn't have the strength to hold the thing down, especially if they shot it on automatic. So I assume that he was just as scared as I was, as he was shooting high. Anyway, without aiming the grenade launcher—it was just laying there—I pulled the trigger. The grenade did not undergo enough revolutions to arm itself, but it did hit the enemy in his face and, I assumed, killed him. I was told the next day by our top sergeant in our company that they did find his body in front of us and his face was horribly disfigured, and they couldn't figure out what had happened to him."

The two men continued to battle to protect the west side for two long hours. Toward the end of the brutal struggle, Phillips looked up to his left and spied a North Vietnamese regular "standing within five feet of the foxhole that we're in." At this point the enemy probably thought the 101st unit was all but defeated. "The guy is just literally standing there. He has a rifle, as best as I can recall, but he is just absolutely standing there, not attempting to do anything. I had a cannister round in the grenade launcher. Now a cannister round is like a super-super-sized buckshot in a shotgun. Well, I shot this guy with this super-sized buckshot, raising him off of the ground two or three feet, and he tumbled down the hill. And to this day, I think that I must have gone out of my mind at that moment. I got Kenneth David's M-16, gave him the grenade launcher, stood up and opened up on the guy I just blew away even though he's obviously very dead." Standing up was the last thing Phillips would have wanted to do if he had been thinking logically. "I felt a searing sensation in my left side. I'm not certain whether it was an AK-47 round or friendly fire that hit me. I was blessed inasmuch as it was just a big hole the size of a softball flesh wound. It didn't hit any vital parts. It didn't hit any ribs or anything. Just hit the flesh and came out."

Ken David's Distinguished Service Cross citation clearly indicates how the usually mild-mannered youth rose to an amazing level of action. "Unleashing a barrage of automatic weapons fire, the private bitterly resisted all enemy efforts to overrun his position. When the enemy began to toss satchel charges in the direction of the wounded allied soldiers, Private David began to shout in a manner which attracted the enemy's attention away from the allied casualties. Refusing to withdraw in the face of the concentrated fire now directed toward him, the private continued to resist the attackers in a determined manner. Although wounded by an exploding satchel charge and running perilously low on ammunition, he tossed hand grenades toward the attackers to effectively counter their fire. Then, after allied reinforcements fought their way to his position, Private David carried a wounded comrade to a sheltered position and returned to the contact area to engage the enemy until they broke contact and fled."[8] Ken David would find himself down to his last clip of ammo when the enemy finally disengaged.

Kenneth Kays, the platoon's rookie medic, must have been briefly immobilized by the explosive and terrible attack, but his initial shock wouldn't last long. Almost a dozen voices began to scream out "medic!" from the darkness. Almost as a reflex, Kays leaped from his foxhole and moved toward where most of the fighting seemed to be occurring. Kays' first moments in combat would be unexpected and brutal. In the midst of the desperate fighting, Gib Rossetter, who continued to fire from his position to the left of Phillips' and David's, recalled seeing 2nd Platoon's medic Ken Kays bolting across the perimeter to help a wounded man when a fat satchel charge landed at the medic's feet. The blast hurled Kays several feet into the air. Just after he landed in a heap, Kays quickly rose and started to run again, but instead of moving smoothly forward, he tumbled end over end. Kays had not realized that the lower portion of his left leg was gone, blown off by the explosion. Rossetter, who had witnessed Kays' horrible wounding, had little time to grieve the loss of their platoon medic. He turned away from the scene and continued firing as more of the enemy pushed up the slope. "I turned back to check on Kays and saw him calmly sitting and putting a tourniquet on the stump of his leg. I had to turn back around but kept trying to watch in both directions. Finally I was able to spin back around. Ken was not sitting there any longer, so I assumed that he had stopped his bleeding and had gone over into the corner where he had stashed some of the other wounded."

Unbeknownst to Rossetter, Kays continued to aid the many wounded. After applying a tourniquet to his leg, the crippled medic, now in almost unendurable pain, hopped and crawled to the fire-swept perimeter, where he quickly gave medical aid to one of the blood-drenched wounded. Years later Kays told his friend Rod Cross, "I thought, after my leg was blown off and I could see the enemy running everywhere around us, that I was going to die. For some reason a great sense of peace came over me with this thought and I decided I would just go out there and help all the people I could before I died."

Kays' unusual upper-body strength now came into play. Once he saw that the injured man was stabilized, Kays managed to drag him to an area of relative safety in the center of the perimeter. At some point early in the melee, Kays had given himself two shots of morphine. The painkiller, in combination with an extraordinary adrenaline rush, now enabled 2nd Platoon's medic to carry out amazing feats of rescue. Kays returned to the middle of the fight in search of other wounded men, and it did not take him long to discover more work. Kays treated another wounded comrade and, using his own body as a shield against enemy bullets and fragments, moved him to safety. Soon, Kays' own blood loss began to affect him, but somehow, amazingly, he continued to seek out and help the wounded. The last that was seen of Kays during the battle, he was "moving beyond the company's perimeter into enemy-held territory to treat other wounded."[9]

In the end, the final fate of 2nd Platoon hinged primarily on gentle Kenneth David's initial determined stand to protect the west side of the platoon's perimeter so that Greek Avgerinos could call in life-saving air support. Greg Phillips' courageous choice to leave the relative safety of the east side and join Ken David ensured that the position would be held. While far from the largest engagement of the war, the battle stands out as highly unusual given the number of awards later passed out for military valor. Perhaps in no other engagement this size, one involving only a platoon of twenty-one men, would the four highest awards for heroism be given. This feature alone suggests the intensity of the struggle that night at Maureen.

Photo of Fire Support Base Maureen taken during the time of the 2nd Platoon's ordeal. Courtesy Don Shaughnessy.

As daylight approached on the morning of 7 May, the enemy melted away. Delta Company members who came to relieve the 2nd Platoon that morning came upon a staggering and unforgettable sight—scattered bodies, some blown apart, almost everyone covered in their own blood or the blood of others. All around lay unexploded satchel charges, with the greatest number extending around Ken David's foxhole. Three or so of the survivors managed to stumble around but due to eardrum damage could not hear well. Some of the living were missing a hand or a leg. Greg Phillips could not shake from his mind the image of Lt. Fletcher's body lying "about six feet behind us that night." It was a horrible vision he would carry forever. Gib Rossetter grew more distressed as he stumbled back to check on his foxhole partner, twenty-one-year-old Bob Lohenry, the Chicago native who had begged Rossetter not to leave the foxhole when the battle started. A stunned Rossetter discovered Lohenry dead of gunshot wounds.

Peter Cook was still alive when pulled from his foxhole. The Massachusetts native had been unable to escape his foxhole when two satchel charges landed inside and the compressed explosion had blown his legs off. Heavily dosed with morphine and with the lower portion of his body covered with a poncho, he was quickly transported to a hospital with the hope that he would arrive before he became totally aware of what had happened. Unfortunately, as he was being loaded, he saw that his legs were missing. Screaming, Cook went into shock and died.

Dale Tauer was in the platoon party that came rushing up to Maureen that morning. "Everyone was shot up, out of ammo. There were bodies all over the place. Some were ours and some were NVA." Many of the enemy lay at the edge of the perimeter. Among the Americans, "there were guys laying over one another in foxholes trying, in the end, to protect their buddies. I was just in horror of what I saw and, being new, I am thinking 'how am I ever going to get over this?'" Remembering the jarring booms of satchel charges from earlier that morning, Tauer was "actually surprised to see anyone alive." Richard Drury, another member of the rescue group, remembered seeing many bodies of enemy soldiers littering the ground as his group drew near the place where 2nd Platoon had made its stand. "We also went to the side of the hill to pick up bodies blown down there." Among the dead enemy was an officer Dean Finch later believed he had "shot off the hill."

Almost all the living among 2nd Platoon suffered critical wounds. Of the twenty-one who made up the group that night, seven died at FSB Maureen. They were Robert Berger, Peter Cook, Lawrence Fletcher, Jose Gonzalez, Lloyd "J. J." Jackson, Robert Lohenry, and Joseph Redmond. So initially shattered by the bitter and intense battle were the survivors of 7 May that twenty years later almost all were unaware that the four highest medals for military valor were awarded to four of 2nd Platoon's twenty-one men: the Congressional Medal of Honor to Kenneth Kays; the Distinguished Service Cross to Kenneth David; the Silver Star to Greg Phillips; and the Bronze Star with "V" device to Steve "Greek" Avgerinos. More than a dozen Purple Hearts were also awarded for wounds received in the battle.

Steve Avgerinos, Greg Phillips, and Ken David, along with a forward observer named Brunson who had his hand blown off while trying to hurl back a satchel charge, were the last of the survivors to climb aboard a helicopter. They were about the only ones still able to walk. As the chopper dipped, then pulled away, the four weary men found themselves too exhausted to look back. Little did they realize how profoundly affected they had been by what they had just endured. At the time they left, however, they were simply thankful to be alive. The pain and torment would come later.

Dick Doyle, who had been recovering in a hospital when his 2nd Platoon got battered, recalled the shock of seeing and talking with the survivors of 7 May as they came trickling in. "They told me the platoon was asleep when the NVA crept up to the perimeter and started the attack by shooting Fletcher. It was also then I heard how my friend Peter Cook had died. Once again there was no opportunity to grieve for the dead. Once again I had been separated from my unit and buddies." A profound case of survivor's guilt soon kicked in on Doyle. Mike Bookser, recovering from combat injuries received at FSB Maureen in late April, was shocked when he came across a distraught Greek Avgerinos in a hospital and heard Greek's incredible story. The tough platoon sergeant told Bookser some of the enemy must have been Chinese as they were so tall. Curt Alexander recalled how Greek shouted at everyone, but then he realized Avgerinos couldn't hear because his eardrums had been severely damaged by satchel charge explosions.

Greg Phillips, Ken David, Ken Kays, and Greek Avgerinos, along with several others of 2nd Platoon, were able to go home because of their severe wounds. This break, however, cut both ways. By being so quickly separated, the young men were robbed of the opportunity to garner understanding about that night. A few of 2nd Platoon stayed and endured the ongoing combat the 101st continued to engage in up through the Ripcord campaign in mid-July. Tony Cox, an Indianapolis youth, came to the field as a new replacement in the platoon on 8 May, just after the horrible firefight. "I remember landing on the LZ and seeing all these bombed out areas and thinking, 'Oh my gosh, this is pitiful.' I remember meeting the guys who were left of 2nd Platoon, Gib, Dean, "Ernie" Banks, and a few others. They seemed pretty devastated, and there was a certain coldness in the air given what they'd been through."

John Smith, who took over what was left of 2nd, experienced the legacy which followed the 7 May firefight. Several stories about that night had already begun circulating, and they soon took on the aura of legend. One asserted the battle had been so traumatic that one of the new replacements in the platoon had died of fright. "The story was when he was removed from the foxhole, there were no wounds to be found. Perhaps they were hidden from sight, but the poor guy's death was a mystery to the survivors, and he never even got to write a letter home. There was an inquiry from his girlfriend or wife after I was there. It had to have been a dreadfully terrifying night."

2nd Platoon member Tony Cox of Indianapolis, Indiana. Cox was instrumental in helping bring former 2nd Platoon members back together. Courtesy Tony Cox.

Even old veterans of combat in 2nd Platoon, such as Dean Finch, balked at ever going back to the haunted fire base. "Maureen was the one thing Finch always seemed serious about," Smith recalled. "It was from him that I learned what had transpired that night, and he didn't laugh when he told me about it. He was also serious when he said he would not return to Maureen. We almost had a showdown over that one. In the end, the showdown never came because our mission was changed. Had that not happened, I am not sure what Dean would have done. I believe he would have simply refused to get off the helicopter, and because I did respect him as an individual, I wouldn't have physically forced him off. However, I would have put him in jail for a very long time for refusing an order in combat."

It was Finch's later judgment that the Americans killed on Maureen that night probably "all died in the first fifteen minutes of the fight. That is why the battle was so traumatic. The damage came all at once." Others in the 2nd, like Finch, also declared they would never go back.

The impact of the terror of that night on the survivors can be seen in several letters Ken David wrote his parents immediately after the fight. The first was written on the day of 2nd Platoon's rescue.

How is everyone at home? Don't worry for me. I'm fine, and please believe me. This letter is to let you know that I'm fine and still alive. About 4:00 A.M. my platoon got hit. I say again; don't worry—I'm okay. I'm at Phu Bai at the hospital. I got some shrapnel in my back, and its out and I'm in A-1 condition. I'm up and walking around. I'm all in one piece. I have all my arms and legs, and I'm okay. All I can say is God was with me that night. I also got a hole in one eardrum and the other one is OK. I am just hard of hearing now, but Doc says it will come back. I don't know where I am to go from here. I might stay in country or go to Japan, and Doc says I might come home so they could operate on my ear—or they might do it in Japan. Anyhow, I'm alive! Yes, I'm alive. But don't worry I'm okay. I'll be ready to go skiing this winter, that is if I come home. Please don't worry, okay? Because I'm okay. All the prayers you have been saying for me have helped me. Seven or eight GI's were killed and a lot of them got arms and legs blown off. Don't worry, I got all mine, thank God. Well, I don't want to talk about it. I want to forget. I'm still shaking a little. I want to forget, so that I'll be okay.

A later bit of Ken David's correspondence hinted at the psychological pain yet to come. "I'll tell you my war story of what happened on the night of 7 May 70 at 4:00 A.M. to the time I got medivaced, but not now. I'll tell you when I come home. I wake up at night and will be scared, or I will dream of that night. I guess in time it will go away. I hope so."

Shortly after Delta Company came that morning to help rescue 2nd Platoon, someone heard a shout from far down the slope. A Delta Company soldier had stumbled upon an incredible scene and signaled for the others to come see. Half-conscious medic Kenneth Kays, minus a leg, lay on top of two wounded men in an attempt to offer protection. The bloodied medic had gone down the slope sometime during the fierce firefight to give aid to his wounded comrades. Now the medic writhed in great pain and hovered near death from profuse bleeding. The stouthearted Kays, however, refused to be placed on a helicopter until the two severely wounded men were placed there also. Then the deathly pale Fairfield, Illinois, man mercifully passed out.

8

Just a Damn Piece of Metal

On 11 May 1970, the *Wayne County Press* carried a short front-page article titled "Fairfield Boy, Kenneth Kays, loses leg in Vietnam battle." The piece noted the young man had been in combat "for no more than a week," but said nothing about the young man's heroic actions.[1] Returning from Vietnam, the former medic traveled to Fitzsimmons General Hospital in Denver, Colorado, to convalesce. Joe Keoughan had heard of his friend's misfortune while in England teaching mountain climbing courses. Traveling to California to continue his vocation, Keoughan left an assignment early to rush to Denver and be with his boyhood friend. Keoughan was not surprised to find the rugged Kays "getting around by hopping." The seven-month stay in Denver, however, turned out to be an ordeal for Keoughan's friend, as Kays endured several operations and was fitted with an artificial limb. If there was a bright spot, it was that Kays would be medically discharged from the service with more benefits than a retired twenty-year veteran would receive. Still, of great concern to Joe Keoughan at the time was a bitterness he sensed in Kays just below the surface. Friends back home such as Rodney Cross soon noticed this as well.

Almost eight months after the battle at FSB Maureen, Kenneth Kays returned home. His arrival was a quiet occasion, and at first it was hoped by family and friends that he would be able to slip back into his old life. His father, John Kays, recalled, "When he got back from the service he seemed normal enough, but I guess the thought that he had lost part of his leg hadn't hit him. Like, he'd go to dances and run around just as if nothing had happened."[2] Then came the first event of several that seemed to carry Kays down into a dark abyss. Ironically, this event involved a great honor. In January of 1971, Kenneth Kays received the nation's second highest award for military valor, the Distinguished Service Cross. The award is an extremely prestigious one, for "the act or acts of heroism must be so notable and have involved risk of life so extraordinary as to set the individual apart from his or her comrades." Townspeople were likely a bit stunned by Kays' honor, especially after all the Woodstock business and the long-haired Kays' extraordinary attempts to avoid going to Vietnam. Being accustomed to eccentrics, though, the Fairfield community quickly embraced what their young neighbor had accomplished. But signs soon emerged that all was not well with the young man.

A photo, taken during an interview about the award in the *Wayne County Press*, displayed a disheveled and bleary-eyed Kays. The accompanying article also captured Kays' growing anxiety. The *Press* reported, "The young Fairfield soldier sat quietly in his mother's living room puffing nervously on a cigarette." Further noted was how Kays, wearing a beard and a dark green T-shirt, nervously studied the award document as he was being interviewed. As for his future, the paper observed that Kays could look forward to having his college paid for by the GI Bill, along with a monthly living expense wage while in school. Kays said, "I think I'll stay around Fairfield a little longer, then go to California for a visit and then on to Europe this summer with some friends. After that, I might like to live in Colorado. Maybe go to school there. It's beautiful country out there, the nicest I've ever found."[3]

Trying to regain his life, Kays did return briefly to SIU. Also, that summer, Joe Keoughan came home and together he and Kays hiked trails and scaled cliffs in the nearby Shawnee National Forest area. "Kenny still had an incredible amount of energy. We hiked the Shawnee Forest trail from one side of the state to the other and climbed rocks." Kays' friend was especially impressed that although he had but one good leg, Kays, with his upper-body strength, was still able to scale the toughest cliffs. During that time Kays struggled to explain his actions at FSB Maureen to his friend. "I just thought 'shit, I'm going to die. Might as well help people.'" Despite the bravado, deep down Kays often simmered with bitterness and anxiety that can be seen in a number of poems and journal entries he kept as an assignment for a writing class at Southern Illinois University when he returned to school. Dark themes often emerged, a primary one being Kays' horrific war experiences. In "Subjective Nam" the young man wrote of the wasted lives for the supposed reason of making people free. "It all a joke," Kays asserted. Kays also contended that it was monstrous for American troops to be encouraged to believe that their enemy was less than human. "Yea those are men out there, but it's hard to admit / So we just call 'em Charlie and try to forget." In another, "Post Mortem," Kays wrote of that awful night at FSB Maureen and how it impacted his life.

> I've seen too much and been too far
> To really love you when you're near
> For horrible visions haunt my mind
> Of bloody death and unchained fear.

> When I hold you in my arms
> I see men who've long since gone
> Guys who helped me through the night
> Blown away before the dawn.
> To men who've shared a bloody hill
> And soaked up fire and lead
> Many words acquire a new meaning
> Like love and friend and God and dead.
> These guys are all real as you
> And now I see that I've died too.

Another subject which emerged in much of Kays' writings was how constraining the educational process had become to the young man. "The students sit with deadened mind / And absorb by rote the written culture / Duplicating unfeeling facts in the dreary, daily, grind," Kays lamented in one piece. Even more alarming were the many poems celebrating the use of drugs. In one, Kays declared his joy in mixing Benzedrine, cocaine, and pot. Other bleak poems suggested Kays' coming breakdown. "My life seems hopelessly divided / Between what is now and what used to be / No continuum to be found / No awareness to set me free." In "World of Black," Kays told of "Prophets" speaking "of the coming fire / While eyeless apes climb funeral pyres." Still, one could discern the inner core of strength and will, one which profoundly reflected his southern Illinois roots, in a poem titled "Chained but Unconquered." Kays declared, "I vowed the system nothing / And wanted nothing in return." The young writer realized however that society stood as a powerful force with which he must battle. Kays went on to observe,

> But they chose to pay my room and board
> In the hope that I would learn.
> They put me in a cage
> And locked the door behind.
> Now that they had chained my body
> they tried to train my mind
> To see through their myopic eyes
> And follow the script their daddies wrote.
> But how could a band of docile sheep
> Hope to train a billy goat
> Thus, never did they smother Kays
> Nor hear the inner cry—Ba Ba

Eventually, Kays dropped out of school again, but given his fierce determination to be a southern Illinois individualist, he might have still weathered the difficult shift back to his home life had it not been for another major event which occurred in October of 1973. Out of the clear blue sky, Kays received notification that he would be awarded the Congressional Medal of Honor. Of the more than a million armed forces members who served during Vietnam, only 239 received this award, and almost 70 percent of those died in the process of gaining it. So potent has been the recognition for this honor that it has often created a burden too great for the receiver to bear. So it would be for Ken Kays. As John Kays would note later, "about the time Kenny got that medal, he stopped talking to me and his mother. He started raising hell and smoking grass."[4]

Perhaps Ken Kays sensed that taking the medal would do him great harm, for at first he balked at going to Washington, D.C., to receive the award. The Kays family told no one locally about the upcoming ceremony at the White House as they begged their stubborn son to cut his hair and beard in preparation for the event. Finally, the elder Kays asked local state politician "Pud" Williams to talk to his son. Williams convinced the young man to go, but Kays would not consent to cut his beard or hair, and as a result of Kays unkempt look, the army refused to let him wear a uniform. Kays ended up as the only one of the nine servicemen who received the medal that day who was not in military garb.

The *Wayne County Press*, in a nice front-page article, reported of their hometown hero, "A 24 year-old Fairfield army veteran, Kenneth Michael Kays received this nation's highest military honor, the Congressional Medal of Honor, at ceremonies at the White House in Washington at 11 A.M. Monday. The young man, son of John and Ethel Kays, 303 North West Ninth, was one of nine Vietnam veterans so honored by President Richard Nixon. . . . Kenneth and his parents flew from St. Louis to Washington Sunday morning, accompanied by an Army major as military escort. He is believed the first Wayne County serviceman ever to receive such an honor." Following the medal presentation, the nine Vietnam veterans were guests of honor at a buffet luncheon hosted by Mrs. Nixon.[5]

Perhaps, recalling all the hassle in the local paper following Ken Kays' journey to Woodstock, the family decided not to talk to the local press about the Washington trek. This led to some hurt feelings, with the *Wayne County Press* demurring, "We got scooped by the wire services and area city papers a bit on the story, but we had been tipped off by a friend eight days before that Kays was to get the Medal of Honor; but the family, when we called 'em, said they had been instructed not to release any story here in advance." Still the paper, and the community, seemed extremely proud of what Ken Kays had accomplished. "We respected their wishes and didn't print the story a week before it happened. But that's of little importance . . . again, a tip of the hat to Kenny!"[6] But the next day the local paper complained, "*The Press* carried a picture of the young honoree and a full

Kenny Kays receives the Medal of Honor at the White House from Richard Nixon. The army refused to let Kays wear an army uniform because of his long hair and beard. *AP Photo courtesy Wayne County Press.*

story Monday. Efforts to reach him for pictures and interviews since his return were unsuccessful. His mother told a *Press* reporter he has been exhausted since his return and is resting at his home here. A community wide observance in honor of the young man is being planned and, at that time, the *Press* will seek to have comments from the young man about the high honor he has brought himself and his home town community."[7]

The parade, however, would not take place. Kays came back home and hid for three weeks in a cabin in the woods, telling a friend at the time, "I can't handle being a hero. I just don't think I've been that brave. Besides being a Medal of Honor man doesn't make me any better than anyone else."[8] The young man's descent into hell had begun.

Many Fairfield folks likely were surprised and pleased at first that one of their own, although an eccentric person, had received such a high national accolade. Few communities could boast of having a living Medal of Honor recipient among them, and many town leaders, as evident by their requests on Kays' return from getting the medal, now hoped Kays would be available for community celebrations such as parades. And what mid-American small town wouldn't have wanted such a sight—a Medal of Honor recipient, with his medal hanging from his neck, sitting in the back seat of a shining convertible, waving to a grateful and happy crowd? Such a thing would have been a pleasant thought for city leaders in that time of national disturbance. Kays' negative reaction, however, surely surprised the townspeople, especially older ones. Not understanding the pressure the medal created for the war-shattered man, many of the older generation in Fairfield quickly perceived Kays' jestings, hesitations, and reserve as a lack of respect. John Kays noted later, for example, that his son acted like the Medal of Honor ceremony "was a joke."[9] Another issue for Fairfield folks may have been Kays' actions at the ceremony itself. At the time of the awards, President Nixon's political situation had grown especially perilous. Awarding nine Medals of Honor would play well for him. Nixon's positive moment seemed to be working well when the first award recipient, former POW Lt. Col. Leo Thoresness, who obtained "an especially strong handshake from Nixon," declared, as he pointed to the president, "he got me out." The bearded, long-haired, unpredictable Ken Kays, however, was another story. When the president first entered the room, Kays alone remained seated. To limit the damage any odd behavior on Kays' part might cause, the Fairfield man was the last to receive his award.[10] A *Washington Post* photographer captured the moment as a shaky Nixon placed the medal around Kays' neck. A local Wayne County native wrote the *Wayne County Press* about the affair, noting, "Just in case someone might be interested in a copy of the *Washington Post*'s coverage of the ceremony honoring the Medal of Honor heroes, here's my copy. The many emotions evoked by this picture of Kenneth Kays and President Nixon should win the photographer a prize."[11] Years later Kays told friends the only reason he went to Washington, D.C., was to "look Nixon in the eye."

As noted by Ken Kays' father, things began to fall apart rapidly for the young Fairfield man after he received the Medal of Honor. In early April of 1974, police officers raided the small greenhouse next to John Kays' residence and found hundreds of small marijuana plants growing in trays. The Kays' house and greenhouse sat across the street from Robert Hawkins, the state's attorney, which added to the anger of local law enforcement. Armed with a search warrant, law enforcement officers also entered twenty-four-year-old Ken Kays' trailer adjacent to the greenhouse and found marijuana seeds. Young Kays himself seemed "indifferent to the proceedings," standing by "as police examined and counted the plants." The *Press* reported Kays "appeared very cooperative to police queries."[12]

Perhaps Kays' status as a war hero brought him a break for his first offense, for which he received a fine of $100 and was placed on one year of probation. A week later, however, police returned to the Kays' greenhouse and found eight more trays of marijuana seedlings. That same day, after a more extensive search, 180 more illegal plants were discovered. At this point Kays declared to the court that growing pot stood as an individual's right, and he asserted to the judge that he "would keep on growing it."[13] Because of Kays' status as a Medal of Honor recipient, his case began to receive national attention. His arrests made the Associated Press wire, and in early May of 1974 Dick Cowan, a freelance writer for the *National Review* who had written several articles dealing with the nation's marijuana laws, hurriedly trekked to Fairfield to offer Kays legal help. Cowan told the *Wayne County Press* he had read about Kays in an Associated Press story in Texas and "thought I ought to come up and see if I could help. If Kenny needs it, the Organization for the Reform of Marijuana Laws will provide him legal counsel." The outsider also emphasized how Kays' Medal of Honor had caused the arrests of the young man to receive "nationwide publicity."[14]

Ken Kays' defiant actions regarding his cultivation and use of pot may have been enhanced by the region's cultural acceptance of the individualist, those like the Shelton brothers, who often lived at the edge of the law. As visitors to the region had long noted, southern Illinois had a long history of celebrating this type of desperado, and another longtime subtle cultural norm in "Little Egypt" concerned one's right to exercise lifestyle choices if they did not bother others. In this sense, Kays was not altogether peculiar for the area. But, unfortunately for Kays, the region and the country at large were experiencing a backlash against the behaviors of the youth counterculture, especially drug use. Jack Vertrees, in one *Press* article, explained, "Efforts are already being made in our state legislature to legalize the use of marijuana. One by one, we see the legalization of these things that for years have been regarded as taboo. We may be the wickedest guy in town, but somehow it all goes against the grain."[15] Another article in the *Press* warned that "the percentage of students now using drugs in our area may pass 50 percent."[16] Numerous other antidrug articles also began to appear in the paper as well.

Regardless of community fears and concerns with drug use, Kays doggedly continued his quest to grow and use pot, even refusing to work with his court-appointed attorney regarding his pending charges. Then, in June of 1974, law enforcement officers discovered a number of marijuana plants growing on Kays' father's property two miles east of Fairfield. In a front-page piece, the *Press* reported, "Kenneth Kays, who has been in a continuing conflict with Wayne County authorities concerning his cultivation of marijuana plants, is a man of his word. After being arrested twice in the last two months on charges of growing marijuana in his father's greenhouse, the Medal of Honor recipient told authorities he didn't agree with the law, and would continue to grow the plants." Authorities found the plants growing "over a 25 X 50 foot tilled patch of ground. Many of the plants had been given close personal attention, and were rooted in little containers in rich potting soil. Others were found growing randomly in the ground, among tomato plants. They were uprooted by the officers."[17] The find, however, was not all that shocking. A week earlier. the stubborn Kays had told an AP reporter of spending the day caring for his plants. Perhaps what did shock the rest of the nation was Kays being committed by his distressed father to a mental health center.

Kays' story now exploded on the front pages of national media and on television. One Associated Press reporter related Kays' side of the story. The young man's worldview, while similar to the counterculture's of the day, was also clearly that of some of his southern Illinois individualist predecessors. "At the heart of Kays' philosophy," explained the reporter, "is the belief that a man must be true to himself, must do what he thinks is right. But first he must be free to find himself, so that he'll know what's right. Marijuana is a tool in the quest. He won't participate in a system that obstructs the search." Kays further told the reporter, "They see my adherence to responsibility as irresponsibility. All they are is what they have been told. What purpose is served by restricting freedom?" Kays went on to assert, "I don't wish to fight, but I'm not going to quit. I will trust to the courts to see that justice is done. My only weapon is the truth. No man has the right to dictate to another." The reporter then explained the other side of the coin, how the patience "of the prosecutor, the sheriff, and the judge are wearing thin. They've tried to debate Kays' beliefs with him. But he can't see it their way. 'They're wrong,' argues Kays. Consequences don't trouble him: 'What's to frighten me? Are they going to send me back to 'Nam?' asks Kays."[18]

Newspapers from coast to coast carried Kays' story. The *Los Angeles Times*, for example, told in early June how the "draft resister–turned medic [who] won the Medal of Honor today has as his battlefield a patch of marijuana near his trailer in Fairfield, Illinois." Two days later the same paper reported Kays "couldn't adjust to being a hero and was growing pot as his part for personal freedom."[19] Such reports seemed glib, failing perhaps to get at deeper problems haunting Kays, such as his deep resentment toward his father, who often maintained a powerful control over his only son's life. A few years later, when Kenny experienced his first mental breakdown requiring institutional care, a counselor visiting the health facility where Kays was brought witnessed the young man stripped bare for his own safety, ranting uncontrollably while hurling his own excrement against the small viewing window in the door. The witness was amazed when he found that the patient was a Medal of Honor recipient. His curiosity piqued, the counselor went out of his way to talk to the personnel working with Kays and was told his explosive anger seemed to spring from unresolved feelings about his father.

The *Chicago Tribune*, *St. Louis Globe Democrat*, and *Washington Star News*, among many other large newspapers, also featured lengthy articles about Kays' situation. Even smaller newspapers, like Missouri's *Sedalia Democrat*, now found Kays' plight of great interest. In a story headlined "Vietnam Hero Fighting in Marijuana Conflict," the paper noted, "Kenneth Kays is not your government issue hero. His victory garden is full of marijuana, and he is determined to keep it as a symbol of his freedom. . . . Today his battleground is a 1,000 square-foot patch near his trailer in this southern Illinois town where he farms the illegal marijuana plants for his own personal use. With practiced ease, he swings down the rows on his artificial leg, hoeing, raking, and tilling. A headband secures his long sun-tinted hair which cascades into his beard." This piece captures well the iconic status the young headstrong man had achieved. News media seemed to be turning him into a caricature of a counterculture hippie while ignoring or perhaps not understanding his extreme personal problems, problems the introverted Kays likely had trouble expressing or understanding himself. More than a few Americans likely sympathized with his efforts. The Sedalia article also captured Kays' struggle with the pressures the Medal of Honor had wrought. "The medal he earned has no value of itself, only the experience it represents, and has often been a source of trouble, he said, bringing him unwanted attention and praise."[20]

Locals grew greatly concerned about Kays' actions and the national attention it drew to Fairfield. The *Press* commented, for example, "The continuing stories on Kenneth Kays, Wayne County's most decorated war veteran, and his breach with the law over growing marijuana, has stimulated nationwide interest among the news media. His first arrest two months ago led to headlines across the nation." Kays' latest escapades, the Wayne County paper reported, brought "an Associated Press reporter, Dennis Montgomery, conduct[ing] a two-hour interview with Kays which was carried nation-wide, including on the front page of the *Washington (D.C.) Star-News*. Harper Barnes, a feature writer from the *St. Louis Post-Dispatch*, was in town Monday seeking an interview. Tuesday, Hal Fisher, a field producer for CBS News, out of Chicago, walked into the *Wayne County Press* office seeking information on the Kays story. Thursday, a CBS-affiliate television station out of Miami, Florida, called the *Press*, also seeking information."[21] In another short article, the local paper noted, "The Kays story is attracting national attention. A Fairfield boy, Jerry Quindry, sent the *Press* a copy of the front page of Monday, June 3, issue of the Washington, D.C., *Star News*, which had a boxed 6-column story on young Kays, including his photo." Jack Vertrees reported, "From Charles Kenneth Johnston, recently out in Los Angeles attending a UAW-CIO convention came a copy of the *Los Angeles Times*, with a big page two story about our town's Congressional Medal of Honor winner and his troubles. That story really got around."[22]

The swelling attention young Kays received only increased the pressure the Vietnam hero now experienced. As reporters flocked to tiny Fairfield to get a story, Kays found himself hounded. A reporter for a St. Louis paper, for example, told of going to Kays' trailer door in hopes of gaining an exclusive interview. After repeated knocks, a disheveled young man in a long beard came to the door. "Inside," the determined reporter explained, "on the floor were mattresses covered with paisley cloth." Kays, however, barred the interloper from going past the door. The frustrated reporter asked Kays if he would discuss the problems faced by Vietnam veterans. This only set the agitated man off. "I've talked all I'm going to talk. I've done all I'm going to do," Kays shouted and slammed the trailer door.[23]

Also of growing concern was Ken Kays' increasingly bizarre behavior and fits of intense rage. On Memorial Day 1974, in the midst of his pot-growing plight, Kays borrowed his father's car and went tearing through town, shouting and honking his horn while taking "several laps" around the town "circuit." He later told a reporter, "I was trying to wake the dead."[24] He further angered police when he belligerently threw away the ticket he received for the strange outburst. A few days later, construction workers building a house heard shouts coming from Ken Kays' trailer and alerted John Kays, who found his son screaming incoherently inside his trailer. The elder Kays again quickly signed a petition to commit his son for medical treatment.

World War II–generation residents of Fairfield, especially veterans, had a difficult time accepting Kays' behavior. Many believed that as a Medal of Honor recipient, Kays had an obligation to act as a role model to the youth. Many also understood that as a Medal of Honor recipient, the lucky young man had greater possibilities for success than the average person. In southern Illinois vernacular, Ken Kays just seemed to be pissing it all away. Kays, in fact, reviled the medal for how it destroyed his cherished privacy. He complained to a neighbor, "You don't know what it's like to walk out these doors, and people are looking at you and wondering if you've got on the same clothes you had on yesterday." Kays also continued to criticize the war. "I don't believe we're accomplishing anything," he explained to a *Wayne County Press* reporter before the war ended. "You can't find them [the enemy]. You have to go out there and wait for them to hit you. And no matter how many you kill, there are always more who will fight you."[25] At first, Kays seemed annoyed by the attention his Medal of Honor brought him. Later he came to wish he had never been selected, telling Rod Cross the award was "just a damn piece of metal." Terry McGaha, a year older than Kays, recalled coming home from several years in the service and being told by some older veterans that "you weren't even in a war, just a conflict." Kays endured the same treatment. Rodney Cross observed of his friend, "Kenny seemed changed when he got back. I think the loss of his leg was especially hard on him. And then the people here in town didn't seem to respect him. So many didn't want to give him credit."

There did appear one letter of support to the editor of the *Wayne County Press* during Ken Kays' initial difficult times. A Korean War veteran wrote, "Please! I beg of you, let this veteran off the hook. Oh sure, reprimand and admonish, but leave him go. Probation is a possibility, of course, but he must not face criminal charges, as it would demoralize him." The writer went on to explain, "I can admit to being an alcoholic since the Korean War. I am 44 years old and well remember how another Medal of Honor Veteran of World War II died, in the gutter—as an alcoholic. His name, 'Ira Hayes,' an American Indian, one of the five who raised the American Flag on Iwo Jima. The point I'm trying to make is no one person knows what I went through—nor what Kenneth Kays had to suffer for our country." The passionate writer ended by proclaiming, "If you saw the 'dead and the dying,' I don't have to explain. If, however, you didn't, please have compassion on this (one-legged) 'Medal of Honor' Man. Booze—pot, what's the difference to one who already saw Hell."[26]

Ken Kays himself now seemed to understand he had severe problems, for in mid-June 1974, he volunteered to receive treatment at a state mental health center in Anna, Illinois. While still profoundly antiwar, Kays had complete respect for his fellow comrades in arms and all others who served in Vietnam. It was during his time at the Anna facility that Kays spotted another patient, a young hippie-looking fellow wearing an army jacket with the Screaming Eagle emblem on the sleeve. Finding out the man had not served in the 101st or even in the military, Kays made him quickly take it off, noting that too many men had suffered wearing that emblem for it to be disrespected.

Mental treatment at this time for the struggling Medal of Honor recipient was less than effective. Not being committed by a court allowed Kays to seek release after a few weeks of care, and Kays took advantage of this circumstance. The young man returned home to Fairfield, where he now endured intense bouts of survivor's guilt. His mother, Ethel Kays, began to find notes lying around the house that her son had written to the dead soldiers he tried to save that night at FSB Maureen. The notes typically apologized "for not having reached them quickly enough on the battlefield to save them." Many years later Kays told a friend that "survivor's guilt is worse than any pain I felt in my leg."[27] Unfortunately, Kays was never able to connect with the other survivors from 7 May 1970. Perhaps he might have found some solace in talking to others who had also endured that night and in finding out the names and the stories of those he saved and tried to save.

In 1976, old friend David Steiner returned from New York City to Fairfield and ran into his Woodstock companion Ken Kays. Steiner had heard wild and obviously untrue rumors that his friend "had developed a messianic complex, had visions, had given his trailer away, had given his Buick Riviera away, was investing in land in Central America, and was a pusher to all Fairfield's teenagers." However, Steiner did grow troubled when he finally saw and talked with his friend. "Kenny was wearing an army fatigue shirt and camouflage hat with a small metal pin in the shape of marijuana leaf on it. He immediately made it known that he had just returned from Anna, the state hospital, for the fifth time. His father had sent him each time and, unless a person goes voluntarily, a week of testing is the most they can legally detain someone."

Kays described his testing at the mental hospital to his friend "as being put in a cage or cell inside a small room where an evaluator would ask a question to which Kenny deliberately calculated his answers to confound or upset the evaluator who would then run into another room; confer with other evaluators; then return with another question." When Kays removed his hat momentarily, Steiner could see that "Kenny had recently shaved his head yet kept his beard. Two days later I would hear he had shaved this off as well and had given an exhausting eight-hour performance of sometimes rhymed, sometimes alliterative free association conversational phrase poetry punctuated by artificial laughter at a Christmas party." Kays confided to his friend that he had "moved his marijuana farming to a secluded rural location and, other than music, his current interests were into ESP, especially as experienced with television. 'The $10,000 Pyramid is a strong show to focus on,' he informed me. He also named several television personalities who provided a strong focus. Kenny summed up his ESP interests by saying, 'I decided to stop reading about it and started doing it.'"

In the late summer of 1979, Kays experienced an especially severe bout of eccentric behavior, this time involving his neighbors. The *Press*, as always, reported the odd and disrupting incident in great detail. "At 5:10 P.M. Sunday, city police were called to the home of Mr. and Mrs. Elwood Campbell, 900 W. Water, who live across the street from Kays' mobile home. The Campbells told officers that they were preparing to back out of their carport when Kays ran across the street screaming at them and waving his arms. They pulled back in the carport and ran over to the home of a neighbor, Mrs. John Hoffee, who was observing the incident from her back door. She let the couple in and locked the door." Kays followed the couple and later picked up a flowerpot and threw it through a door glass. Kays then nonchalantly walked back to the Campbells' home and got in their car and drove off. Police officers had to take him into custody by force. "At the jail, he allegedly tore up his mattress and set fire to it. Earlier in the afternoon another passer-by reported that Kays shouted at her, motioning for her to stop. She did not. A charge of marijuana possession is currently pending against Kays from an incident resulting in his arrest several weeks ago. He has been arrested a couple of other times in recent years for cultivating marijuana."[28]

Again Kays' situation drew national attention. Perhaps most powerful of all the media reports was a piece done by *Chicago Tribune* writer Ellen Ogintz, who told of Ken Kays' sad plight. "Kenneth Kays stared bleary eyed from behind the bars of his cell in archaic Wayne County Jail. 'I'm going to be 30 next month and I guess I don't have much to show for it,' he said, talking through the small window of the hot, smelly cell. But Kays has more to show for his first 30 years than most men do for their lifetimes. He is a hero, a Congressional Medal of Honor winner. Six years ago, he stood proudly next to his parents as President Nixon placed the heavy gold medal around his neck." Explaining how Kays had returned from fleeing to Canada to become a medic so that he "might help people," the reporter went on to say, "Now he needs help—more than he ever has in his life, he admits. He faces a myriad of charges from disorderly conduct to possession of marijuana and auto theft. The real problem though is Kays' mental health." Family members and townspeople believed, "the army, Vietnam and even the medal" contributed to Kays' growing problems. Indeed, excerpts from the young man's diary indicated that the status which came with the medal may have pushed Kays over the edge. "After this high point in my life," Kays wrote, "there isn't much left for me to do, or so it seems. Depression has become a large part of my life."[29]

Another emerging problem for the struggling ex-medic involved his relatively generous army pension, which allowed him not to work. Kays refused to get a job, although he occasionally talked about becoming a doctor or paramedic. Perhaps harking back to his Vietnam experiences, Kays bought an old beat-up ambulance and told people he planned on starting an ambulance service. He never did, and the sight of him driving around in the dilapidated vehicle further added to the town's concern for the young man. By 1979, Kays had isolated himself in his trailer where he spent the day listening to music, strumming his guitar, reading books on religion, writing poetry, and smoking dope.

Local town leaders and worried citizens were once more concerned about the struggling man, as one *Press* report of Kays' court hearing clearly shows. The article described how Kays "sat down at a table with his court-appointed attorney, Neal Laws, Jr. There were brief bits of conversation between the two, and once, a smile on Kenny's face, and that chuckling sound which is his occasional trademark. His reddish-hued hair was long, down to his shoulders. Across, at another table, sat States Attorney Robert J. Hawkins, a folder of papers in front of him. In the front row for spectators, his father, John Kays." The judge noted a state motion hearing to have Kays examined as to his fitness to stand trial and that this had been ordered. Ken Kays' father, John Kays, was called as a witness by Hawkins and indicated that over the past several months his son "has had problems" and at times was irrational. "I don't know what happens . . . he'll be rational at times . . . then he'll have yelling spells . . . he'll take off suddenly, paying no attention to me . . . I think he needs medical help," the elder Kays said, speaking in a quiet voice. Judge Whitmer asked young Kays if he had anything to say. Kenny answered quietly, "No." The judge, noting the psychiatrist's findings, found Kays unable to understand the charges against him and unable to help in his own defense, and he ordered the Congressional Medal of Honor winner to be conveyed to the custody of the Illinois Department of Mental Health. As the hearing ended, John Kays approached the bench and asked Judge Whitmer, "'Will they be able to give him the treatment that he really needs at Chester?' Judge Whitmer replied that they would, reassuring Mr. Kays 'that they will give your son the best care the state has to give.' The father added a final word, 'We'll try it there then . . . and see.'"[30]

Press columnist Jack Vertrees also showed great concern for the troubled man, declaring, "People are concerned about Kenny Kays. We've gotten phone calls from New York and California, as well as Chicago, by people who are concerned that every effort be made to help Kenny recover himself to a less hectic life. From Mrs. Charles Simpson, out of Big Bear City, California, way, a plea that Kenny's cause be pursued and a concern that a much decorated veteran needing help so much should be sitting in the county jail." Before the 1979 episode ended, Kays' situation became something of a political issue when one Illinois candidate for the U.S. Senate asked both President Carter and Governor Thompson to free Kays from the mental health center where he had been sent for treatment. The *Press* reported that Democratic senate candidate Anthony R. Martin Trigona asked both President Carter and Governor Thompson "to pardon Fairfield veteran Kenny M. Kays, who won the Congressional Medal of Honor in Vietnam and who has been confined to a mental institution because of shell shock and combat fatigue. 'I think it is criminal of the state of Illinois

Things fall apart: A struggling Kenny Kays shortly before he took his own life.
Courtesy Randy Reed.

to prosecute someone who is obviously ill, but who is not mentally ill or 'crazy' in terms we normally think,'" the senate candidate lamented. "Kays is suffering from post-combat shock, and confinement in the county jail or the Chester 'Hospital,' which is also a jail, will not help him."[31]

In 1985, Kays was once more released to his family's care. The family itself, however, was rapidly falling apart. His mother, Ethel, died by her own hand after enduring a lingering illness in 1981, leaving seventy-four-year-old John Kays to care for his troubled son. In 1985, after a lingering ordeal with cancer, the elder Kays shot and killed himself in a room next to where his son sat. The details of the event suggest how unhinged Kenny Kays had grown. After one especially long session of complaint by John Kays regarding his physical discomfort, the son said, "There's a gun in the next room. If you feel that way why don't you just shoot yourself?" The weary John Kays did just that.

The next six years became one lonely downward spiral for Ken Kays, as smoking pot became the center of his life. Friend Rod Cross recalled seeing Kays "with two joints lit at once." He often spent the evening before he went to bed rolling a number of joints for the next day. There was also more bizarre behavior. John Keoughan, who served with the Fairfield fire department, remembered going out on a call one night. When Keoughan and the other firefighters arrived they found Ken Kays' vehicle in flames in the road and spied Ken Kays "laying on his stomach in the middle of the road leisurely watching a small battery-operated television while his vehicle burned." There were legions of other odd bursts of sometimes violent behavior for the next several years as Kays grew more withdrawn and eccentric. When violent, the powerfully built man could be an almost impossible handful. Then there were the times when Kays' violent behavior would suddenly shift. Once, when the sheriff and a deputy were trying to load a struggling Kays into a squad car, Kays' artificial leg accidentally came off in the deputy's hand. This made Kays laugh so hard he fell to the ground.

Kays also grappled to try and balance the conflicting feelings he had about the medal. On one hand, he displayed it on his living room wall. (Kays now lived in a small house once owned by his parents.) Conversely, he often complained about the trouble the award had brought him. Rod Cross recalled how Kays would remark that "he had what he called just a damn piece of metal Richard Nixon gave him for a war nobody believed in. Often, he told me, the medal was a worthless piece of shit that stared at him every day."

Ken Kays still had many good days. Friends valued his wit. A classmate, Mike Pottorff, talked to Kays for a long time at a class reunion and recalled Kays "being just as pleasant and intelligent company as a person could ever want." Friend Rod Cross remembered, "There was this family who lost everything in a fire. Kenny told me one day—'Rod come go with me' and we went and put a money order for several hundred dollars in their mailbox. He did this kind of thing several times. Few people know about that side of Kenny." Neighbor Jon Simpson and his family grew especially close to Kays in the last few years of the troubled man's struggles, finding him good company and an intelligent, soft-spoken man. "Kenny could have a wicked sense of humor," Jon Simpson recalled. "Once he said, 'One thing I save on is socks' and he pointed to his artificial leg and laughed."

Sadly, Kays' extreme actions were the ones most remembered. As with the popular Shelton gang stories, almost every Fairfield resident would eventually come to have a Kenny Kays tale. Gary Short recalled when as a young child, for example, he and several others were "playing at Jerry Tullis' house at the intersection of Southwest Fourth and King Streets when this man drove by in a car. He was wearing a full beard, and he just looked at us. It was freaky. He had this crazy look in his eyes. I will never forget it."[32] Only later did Short learn the wild-looking man was a war hero. Other stories of Kays walking into a local eating place and grabbing a stranger's sandwich to take out a bite or Kays taking off his artificial leg and scaring a group "of little old ladies" at a local fast food joint would later be told as well. Jon Simpson saw his neighbor declining and encouraged him to get help. "Just before the end he told me 'Jon, I just can't go on this way.'" Another regional Medal of Honor recipient, Sammy L. Davis of Flat Rock, Illinois, attempted to help Kays during those last dark days, but he found his efforts came too late. Sadly, Davis recalls, "Kenny suffered from classic PTSD [post-traumatic stress disorder]. He removed himself from most of his friends and hid in his house. I tried to get him to allow me to go inside, but he said he just wanted to be left alone. If someone will not accept help, there's little a non–family member can do."

Operation Desert Storm occurred in early 1991. Over the Thanksgiving holiday of that year, Kenneth Kays took his own life. The *Wayne County Press* carried a detailed story in early December about Kays' unusual death. "While most families were celebrating Thanksgiving last Thursday, Kenneth M. Kays, Wayne County's most decorated war veteran—the county's only recipient of the Congressional Medal of Honor—apparently decided to take his own life. Kays, 42, was found dead shortly before 10 A.M. Friday by a former high school friend, Joe Keoughan, of San Diego, who was in town visiting his parents." Keoughan had visited with Kays on Thursday, then went back to Kays' home Friday morning to see how his old friend was doing. "Keoughan was angry with what he found. He could not believe Kays had chosen to exit life in that manner. Coroner Bob Johnson said Kays was found in the living room of the home, with a coat hanger around his neck, hanging from a wall-mounted bookcase." The *Press* also reported that "authorities found a plate on the table containing a small quantity of marijuana cigarettes. An ash tray was nearby, loaded with cigarette butts. . . . In the last year, Kenneth Kays had been living an extremely lonely life." Explaining his war heroism, the paper ended the article, bleakly noting, "During the years after the war, Kenneth Kays suffered through emotional trauma and depression and had been involved in drug use. He was arrested a couple of times for growing marijuana plants and he was treated frequently for emotional disorders in state institutions. He was never married."[33]

Ken Kays' funeral and burial was a simple affair. His remains were cremated. City Alderman Doug Gowler remembered being upset because "city officials did not close City Hall, nor did they send a representative to the gravesite." Neighbor Jon Simpson grew upset at what he thought was the small attendance of military personal for a "Medal of Honor winner." At least most Fairfield folks probably felt Ken Kays had at last found peace.

A week later a jury ruled Kays' death a suicide. "Kays had used a coat hanger which he had attached to a wall mounted bookcase and then kicked out a chair on which he was standing."[34] Not everyone concluded Kays had taken his life. There were rumors of missing money, drugs, and the valuable Medal of Honor, which had hung on his living room wall. Whatever the cause, a deluge of letters to the editor of the *Press* soon followed regarding the local papers' reporting on Kays' suicide. One person wrote in from Georgia lamenting, "I was so upset and so angry when I opened my *Press* yesterday and read the obituary on Kenny Kays. . . . Where is the concern, the compassion that this country once possessed? I went all through school with him and talked to him a lot. Kenny was witty, smart, and could always make you laugh." The upset writer then moved on to Kays' war experiences. "Well, Wayne County was sure proud of Kenny Kays when he put our little home town on national television and received the highest honor that could be bestowed upon a soldier of war. I know Kenny had some emotional problems after the war, but thousands of men did. Kenny's only mistake—or rather misfortune, that I see—was that he was different from other people." Finally, the letter concluded, "Kenny Kays saved a lot of men's lives during the war, at the risk of losing his own. For that, he got a chunk of metal and no understanding or help from the people at home he had known all his life. Well, my hat goes off to Kenny Kays wherever he may be and I hope he finally found the peace of mind that his life wouldn't give him. He will be remembered in my prayers."[35]

Another writer from Florida admonished Fairfield citizens, "After reading the write-up in the *Wayne County Press*, I am furious. I would think that Wayne County's most decorated war hero would deserve something a little better. But then again Wayne County was never proud of Kenny Kays. If anything, most people had nothing but ridicule for him."[36] Perhaps the most upset writer was Kays' young neighbor Jon Simpson, who asserted, "I have been a neighbor and friend to Kenneth Kays for eight years. I have seen the good and the not so good in this time span. My family and I are saddened by his death. This brings me to the reason for writing this article. Personally, I found the printed muck to be in very poor taste. I also wonder where you got the photograph. My feelings about this matter are, if you [the *Press*] are going to write an article labeled 'Taps For Hero,' write such an article and leave out all the muck! I hear the Evansville paper had a very appropriate write up for such a hero. I wonder how many people could have been as courageous and unselfish as Kenneth Kays under the same circumstances he was faced with on May 7th, 1970."[37] Sadly, Kays' Medal of Honor was never recovered by the family. One family member wrote an open letter to the *Press* soon after Kays' burial, begging for its return. To this day, the medal's whereabouts are unknown.

9

Back in the World

A few years after Kenneth Kays' lonely death, some of his former high school classmates began to talk of doing something to honor their friend. Together, the group raised enough money to purchase a small but attractive brass plaque and place it on the brick archway that graced the courthouse square. But the renewed interest in Kays did not occur without controversy. The largest newspaper in the region, the *Evansville Courier and Press*, told of the tension Kays' memory still produced in his hometown. "Just about everybody in Wayne County old enough to remember the Vietnam War has a Kenny Kays story. Unfortunately, most of the stories revolve around Kays' hard drinking, drug-addicted postwar life that ended on Thanksgiving 1991, when at age forty-two, he hanged himself. Except for his loyal friends—many of them from the Fairfield High School class of 1967—few can tell you the real story of Kays' remarkable life, and how he earned the Medal of Honor at Thau Thien province in Vietnam. . . . Back home in Fairfield, Kays was no hero. Even other war veterans rejected him and openly opposed plans to place a plaque on the Veterans Arch in front of the county courthouse to commemorate Kays' heroism."[1]

Despite the concerns of some people, letters to the editor of the local paper, which notably increased in mid-2002, clearly showed support for recognizing Kays' heroic actions in some way. Gary Short wrote, for example, "There is a national hero buried in Maple Hill Cemetery. For one day in this young man's life he exemplified all that is good in human nature. My first encounter with him was in the early 70s, early into his ordeal. We were children playing in a yard and a strange man was driving around and around the block staring at us with a wild look in his eyes. We were yelling at him in our innocent way. My dad told me he was a veteran who had been 'messed up' in the war; a war that would eventually kill him." Short added, "If you asked the average person in Fairfield about this hero, their reaction would be a blank, unknowing stare. But, he is not unknown to people outside of Wayne County."[2]

Mark Tipps argued that an appropriate sign should be placed at the town's city limits honoring Kays. "When I drive into Fairfield the first thing I notice are signs. . . . signs that are well-deserved, full of pride, accomplishments, and self-recognition. We have a sign for a fiddle player, we have a sign for an honorable hometown senator that served in a state far away (he also has a plaque in our courthouse), a sign that resembles an advertisement with the owners' name on it, Boy Scouts, bodybuilders, Jaycees, Rotary, Lions Club, Mules, Mayor, Governor's Award, etc." The writer went on to observe there were no signs honoring Ken Kays. "Honor and forgive a man who put duty, honor, and country above himself. Welcome to Fairfield, Home of Congressional Medal of Honor recipient, Kenneth Kays."[3]

Perhaps the most in-depth letter came from a former native who wrote from Minnesota explaining,

> I feel that I must lend my voice to the call for a memorial for Mr. Kenneth Michael Kays, Congressional Medal of Honor recipient. I knew him as Kenny. Kenny's story is unique, complex, and very interesting. Kenny was well educated, not with a college degree, but with a wisdom that would appear to come from nowhere. His remarks, after reflection, were remarkably relevant and thought provoking. I have seen clippings from the Wayne County Press illustrating that Kenny was active in academic extracurricular activities in his youth. Kenny was also an accomplished musician and guitar player. Kenny taught me several songs when I was learning how to play. Kenny, along with Rodney Cross, and another local man, made the long journey to become a part of history at Woodstock back in 1969. Kenny had a spirit of adventure that was self evident. Kenny was a modest man, never bragging and seldom even mentioning "the war." Whenever I would make some comment about what he gave to our country, he would always reply, that "others gave more, much more, and they never came home." I remember that once I asked Kenny if he thought there should be a monument built for him in Fairfield. His modest reply was a simple "no." Kenny named a couple of other local Fairfield boys who didn't make it back. Kenny never forgot the men that never came home. Kenny came home. According to the story, though, he wasn't the same. How could anyone expect him to be? What if Kenny had not come home? I respectfully submit that there is little doubt that Kenny would have been honored somehow before now. But some will say, "Vietnam was an unpopular war," at least that is what we've been taught. Again I ask, "Is that a sufficient reason to forget Kenny?" Forgetting Kenny is forgetting all of the boys and men who did not forget about their country, their pride and their honor. I appreciate the efforts of others writing in and reminding us all of something we should not have ever forgotten. I believe it is interesting to note, that we are all much younger than Kenny would be if he were still here. I ask, where are

the voices of those Kenny's age and older, those survivors of America's other wars, those classmates and friends. Certainly, many of them knew Kenny when he was a fine, intelligent, young man growing up in Fairfield. Before the war, before coming home, before Vietnam. Therefore, I ask, "Who will help us commemorate this hero, our hero who came home?"[4]

State and local political power broker Robert "Pud" Williams joined in the debate, writing to the *Press* in the summer of 2003. Williams had been called upon by Kays' parents back in 1973 to try and convince the defiant young man to go to Washington, D.C., to receive the Medal of Honor. "I have always been a little perplexed at the controversy surrounding Kenny, so I will not waste any time speculating on why there was such a variety of feeling about Kenny Kays or how Kenny Kays felt about everyone else, because I don't know. . . . For a long time I did not hear much about Kenny Kays except gossip and what I read in the *Wayne County Press*. And then a few years ago, I heard he had committed suicide. I don't believe it really surprised me. I remember thinking peace has finally come to Kenny and all the talk and controversy will be gone. I was wrong." Pointing out the turmoil created when Kays' high school classmates placed the small plaque honoring Kays on the veterans arch, Williams asserted, "The Kenny Kays I intend to remember answered his country's call and when all the chips were down during a ferocious battle in Vietnam, he rose above, above, and above, the call of duty. The Kenny Kays I knew died on that battlefield, but his heart beat on for years, until he off-switched himself. I feel great respect for the Class of 1967 and I will always be proud and grateful. I also will always admire Kenny Kays, and I forgave him his transgressions years ago. Let's put Kenny to rest."[5]

The truth regarding Ken Kays and the Fairfield community is a complex one. Certainly Kays' disruptive actions over the years were more than a little extreme. Still, as classmate Mike Pottorff, the town's fire chief, has observed, many would like to see Ken Kays "reintroduced to Fairfield as a true hero." Pottorff eventually hopes to see "something permanent honoring Kays—perhaps a display in the library featuring the medal, pictures of Kenny in his uniform and the real story of his heroism."[6] More recently, local historian Judith Puckett, in a *Press* column piece on Kays, explained, "Somewhere we've forgotten that heroes were never perfect. They couldn't be—they're too much like the rest of us. . . . They are not turned into semi-gods by their heroism. Their heroism is a challenging reminder of the bravery, the compassion, the courage, the loyalty, and the selflessness that is possible in human beings in spite of our frailties."[7] As of this writing, however, besides the small plaque on the arch at the Wayne County courthouse, Fairfield has yet to place any signs of acclaim in Kays' behalf.

While the community of Fairfield struggles with what, if anything, to do about Kenny Kays' heroism, the survivors of 2nd Platoon, Kenny Kays' comrades from that fateful night at FSB Maureen, and their friends and families have experienced their own brand of torment. The lament of one relative of a soldier killed at Maureen can be found in an anonymous poem dedicated to Lloyd "J. J." Jackson, which appears on a Vietnam memorial website. Jackson had been the 2nd Platoon machine gunner and had been killed at the onset of the FSB Maureen battle. The poem reads:

> A poet, musician, and gentle soul.
> Your loss diminishes the world and darkens the nighttime sky.
> You never backed down. You always stood tall.
> You are missed and loved.
> For as long as I am me,
> And you once were,
> You will live, safe in my heart.

Dick Doyle, who missed the 7 May battle but continued to endure the senseless fighting the 101st faced in Vietnam in late 1970, found life almost unbearable as he wound up his tour. "In the last four to five months I was very withdrawn, especially after most of my platoon was wiped out on May 7th, 1970, so I made few friends, nor cared to. There was no trust and actually a great deal of disdain for people, especially the younger ones who often seemed to act as though the war was a big adventure. I was nearly twenty-five years old at that time and saw things in a different light."

Upon his return to Vermont, Doyle continued to face difficulties. "I can hardly put into words about how I felt regarding war—what a monumental waste before and during my tour in Vietnam. Afterward, I'm ashamed to say that I fell into that passivity mode that many Vietnam vets did once they had survived it. Thousands of soldiers were killed after my return, but the numbing effects of being there and surviving didn't allow me to care. I did my time, now it was someone else's problem to make it through. I feel very bad about that now, reflecting back on it." The fall of Saigon to the North in 1975 further agitated Doyle. "My first huge wake-up call occurred when Saigon/South Vietnam fell to the Communists in '75. That whole televised scenario first brought shock that the South crumbled so quickly, then irrepressible anger that the finality of the war had arrived, and all the lives lost and the maiming there were for nothing. I spent quite a few days as an angry person, with fits of crying, just not believing what I was seeing. I basically took my experiences and my thoughts of those I served with (with a few exceptions) and tucked them away for twenty or more years and became a 'closet vet' except when the memories would come back to haunt me at night in flashbacks and in my dreams."

Much of Doyle's sadness involved the death of his friend Peter Cook at FSB Maureen. In 1994 Doyle visited Bennington, Vermont, where one of the several portable replicas of the Vietnam Memorial in Washington, D.C., was touring the country, to find Cook's and other names of men he knew. "The man in front of me, a stranger, had just laid a floral wreath down and said 'here's to you Peter Cook.' I was stunned and asked him if he knew Peter." The stranger had been a friend of Cook's and explained to Doyle that Peter Cook's hometown was only twenty miles away. Doyle drove to North Adams, Massachusetts, and found his friend's grave, and he later wrote to the Cook family. "My wife and I drove to meet them. A lot of tears were shed. This was the beginning of my relationship with the family." In 1996, Doyle and Cook's father Roy presented a large framed picture of Peter to the VFW post named after Doyle's dear friend. "Roy Cook was beaming with pride." Doyle would remain especially close to Roy Cook until the older man's death. Today, Doyle keeps a photo of his friend "in the left hand top drawer of my desk. I see it every time I open that drawer and find it keeps me grounded, keeps my memories of Peter and his father alive."

Gib Rossetter, like Doyle, endured more time in Nam after the May 1970 battle, then returned home to find that the war in Vietnam was already a sore spot. "When I came home from Vietnam, the president of the local bank, whose son was a friend of mine, was walking down the street towards me. He was about thirty or forty feet away, and he looked up and saw me and immediately crossed the street to the other side. He didn't even acknowledge me. I found people didn't accept me now that they knew I'd been in Vietnam. I went into the closet and never talked about Vietnam until twelve years ago." During this time Rossetter threw his medals "into a field and didn't tell anyone I was a veteran." While the Michigan native saw much more combat after the Maureen fight, over time it was Rossetter's experience at FSB Maureen which seemed to haunt him the most. "I was at Ripcord, which was longer and came after the fight on Maureen, but it was that night on May 7 that really continued to rip at me."

Greg Phillips returned to Alabama where he became successful in sales. The hard-charging Phillips had little time to think or feel about anything regarding his Vietnam days. Still, at times, some memories broke through. Once, for his church, Phillips, along with other veterans, wore his lapel service ribbons to a meeting which highlighted the service of the congregation's veterans. The minister realized the significance of Phillips' Silver Star and asked the Vietnam vet to tell about it. Phillips grew upset and found he could not talk about it. Later, in a piece written on his high school alumni website titled "Every day was a Monday," Phillips discussed in general terms his experiences in Vietnam. "From time to time, the prospect of death really didn't seem so bad. . . . I continuously agonized about the actual combat. To this day, combat is a topic I have never discussed with anyone and never will. I'll keep those 'Mondays' to myself." Until then, Phillips had "never discussed his combat experience with anyone. I think about the Maureen battle almost every day and have played it over and over in my mind thousands of times—could I have done something different to have saved more lives? Could I have gotten to the hardest-hit area faster than I did? Why did I go over there without thinking?"

Upon his return home, Greek Avgerinos struggled to adjust to civilian life. "I didn't work right away and was drinking pretty heavily. My wife said I tried to strangle her in my sleep one night. The nightmares lasted a long time, and it was hard to sleep without being loaded with alcohol. I didn't talk a whole lot about what happened. As a matter of fact, it was not until four or five years later that I was able to tell a priest what happened that night. After fourteen years I was finally able to say out loud what I thought and felt. He explained why I felt the way I did, and that 'survivor guilt' was very common in war veterans." Another priest Avgerinos had known in high school "had a parish in Washington, D.C., and when I had a business trip, I made arrangements to meet with him also. He took me to the Vietnam Veterans Memorial for my first time. I didn't make an effort to keep the names and faces fresh in my mind since that night and now I sincerely regret it. I can understand what Kenneth Kays must have gone through because it was hard enough for an unknown like me just having to deal with the fact that I couldn't save the lieutenant. I couldn't get to the other men who needed help, and I couldn't go back and change anything I said or did that night." Avgerinos endured an especially hard bout of survivor's guilt. "I've played the tape in my head over and over again a thousand times and blamed myself each time. I should have made the rounds and alerted everyone when Little David told me what he heard. I should have suggested that we go with two on and one off instead of one on two off. I should have woke Lieutenant Fletcher up and told him what was going on. I should have been able to save everyone's life, and I didn't."

Like his brothers in the 101st, Ken David too endured a troublesome return to the world. He bought a shotgun—not for safety, but for comfort. "We went to sleep holding our guns and strapped with grenades, and then they expect us to sleep in a regular bed," the Ohio native explained to a local newspaper reporter. In 2003, a local paper told of his long odyssey toward reconciliation. "Kenneth J. David said he can remember waking up nights standing in the hallway of his Niles home holding a shotgun. Loud, sudden noises, David said, would send him lunging for the floor. The odor of burnt toast set fire to emotions deep inside David's gut, emotions left kindling for years after his return home from Vietnam. 'It was just a reaction,' David, 53, said. 'Burnt toast smelled of satchel charges and burning flesh.'"

It wasn't until fifteen years after coming home and four years of counseling that Ken David began to readjust to life "and mourn the members of his platoon who were killed on May 7, 1970—the same day David was injured from a rocket-propelled grenade." The Ohio native reported how he "couldn't cry when I came back from Nam. 'It was an emotion the government took away from me. About six months into my counseling, the counselor hit a nerve, and I couldn't stop [crying] for at least two hours. He had to cancel his next session.'" Little David's final step to recovery occurred when he visited the Vietnam Veterans Memorial in Washington, D.C., where the names of the men in 2nd Platoon are engraved. Because the seven men from the platoon died on the same day, their names are etched close together. "At that spot," David told his hometown newspaper, "I was able to lay to rest of my demons from the war. I couldn't carry those guys with me anymore."[8]

Perhaps the most helpful agent for healing among 2nd Platoon survivors were group reunions, which began to take place in the early 1990s. It was at these numerous meetings where, amazingly enough, many 2nd Platoon survivors first heard about Ken Kays' medal. Tony Cox recalled how several former 101st members attempted to find Kays and see how he was doing, but uncovered a mournful story instead. "Paul Mueller, Merle Delagrange, and I were talking about how we could get in touch with other guys, and suddenly thought, 'Well, let's see if we can find Ken Kays.' It was kind of hard to do. Paul sold ads for the yellow pages, so that was part of his territory down there around Fairfield, Illinois. So in the process of getting in touch with some of the guys we had been over there in Vietnam with, we started having reunions, and we found out where Ken Kays lived."

Sadly, the reclusive Kays did not have a phone. "We didn't have any way of getting in touch with him. We were trying to figure a way to look for him in what was probably the summer of 1991. I think we discussed this when Fire Base Indy [a Vietnam veterans reunion in Indianapolis] was going on in June of '91. I had never thought of asking Sammy Davis [Medal of Honor recipient from the same area as Kays] if he knew him. In June of '91, I wish I would have. Because Ken took his life on November 29, 1991." Sammy Davis later explained to Tony Cox and the group how he had attempted to help the struggling Kays. "Ken wasn't very receptive to Sammy. Ken's drug problems were pretty bad at that time. I always felt kind of bad about that. We were trying to get in touch with all of the guys, and it's kind of ironic that a man who was a recipient of our nation's highest award for military valor didn't have anybody there to help him. Here he did save lives and no one could help him save his."

Cox later made a pilgrimage of sorts to Ken Kays' hometown to try and find out more about the 2nd Platoon hero. "Once, on my way back to Indianapolis from St. Louis, I stopped in Fairfield, Illinois, for the first time. This was probably in the summer of '92. I wanted to pay my respects to Ken Kays. I went into the town, and people weren't too receptive to any of the questions I was asking. I remember especially going to the VFW post there, and I was really surprised to know that no one knew anything about him, and maybe didn't want to know." The determined Cox ended up going to the county courthouse, "and there was a lady in there who was pretty nice. She told me about what happened with him and how he had been and how he had been acting around town. I guess he didn't have any friends. Except for maybe drug dealers."

Finally the Indianapolis man visited Ken Kays' grave. "There was no headstone at the time. The VA hadn't put one up yet. I remember going back whenever I'd go out—I probably went to St. Louis a couple more times after that and, the last time I went was in the year 2001. I visited his grave then and went through Fairfield, didn't ever notice any signs there stating this was the home of Ken Kays, Medal of Honor recipient. They had a sign there recognizing a baseball player whose name I can't remember. I guess maybe Ken burned a lot of bridges there in Fairfield."

What Ken Kays felt he was unable to do in life, help others at FSB Maureen, he ironically accomplished in death. Ken Kays' heroism became a kind of healing point for the survivors of 2nd Platoon. Dick Doyle recalled, "In 1994 I was assigned to Fort Sam Houston, Texas, in the army reserves and went there for my two weeks of annual training and ended up working in MEDCOM HQ, medical command headquarters for all medical forces in the army. So one day I started prowling around the building on my lunch hour, and on the first floor where many of the 'brass' had their offices, I noticed a gallery of pictures were hung in the hallway, all the Medal of Honor recipients from the medical field. I found Ken's citation and picture, so I came back the next day and stopped a passerby and had my picture taken in my uniform next to Ken's citation." Gib Rossetter wished only "to have seen Ken Kays again, back in the world, not that I could have made a difference in his life, but he certainly made a difference in mine." Rossetter's feelings are shared by all the 2nd Platoon men.

Three of the 2nd Platoon's survivors did not get the benefit of those first Delta Company meetings. Greg Phillips, Steve Avgerinos, and Ken David had not stayed in contact with each other or with any of their old comrades. Consequently, after more than thirty years they still knew absolutely nothing about the other men they had served with or that their medic had received the Medal of Honor for his actions at FSB Maureen.

Determined and successful, Greg Phillips thought of himself as pretty much unconnected to his war experiences. In his mind, he had simply gone on with his life, but fate, as it so often does, intervened. Phillips had been surfing the Internet at work when he decided to see if there might be a site available on the 101st Airborne. "The office was about to throw me a 55th birthday party. I found the 101st Medal of Honor winners and was going over them, and Kays' name and company caught my eye. I opened his page up and was shocked at what I saw. I couldn't even enjoy the party after that." Phillips had been completely unaware of Ken Kays' award. Reading the citation released many difficult and painful memories.

Phillips also found Dick Doyle's e-mail address on the site and quickly contacted him. From Doyle, Phillips found out about this Kays book project and, through his typical determination, located Ken David, the radioman Phillips had bravely gone to that night thirty some years before to help defend 2nd Platoon's perimeter. Steve "Greek" Avgerinos, the 2nd's platoon sergeant, was much harder to find. Phillips' perseverance, however, again paid off. When Greek received the e-mail, he promptly responded to Phillips, writing back, "I'm amazed that you found me." Eventually, Avgerinos discovered that being able to reconnect with Phillips and David was amazingly healing. "When my wife gave me the first message from Greg via e-mail, she was worried and asked me if I was okay. I said I was fine and hung up the phone. I got halfway down the first set of stairs in our bi-level home and lost it. I sat on the steps and cried for what I couldn't forget and for what I couldn't remember. A week later I talked to Little David on the phone and he said something that helped me more than anything else anyone had said since that night on Maureen. He simply said, 'Welcome home, Greek.'"

Appendix A

Congressional Medal of Honor Citation for
Kenneth M. Kays

For conspicuous gallantry and intrepidity in action at the risk of his life above and beyond the call of duty. Pfc. (Then Pvt.) Kays distinguished himself while serving as a medical aid man with Company D, 1st Battalion, 101st Airborne Division near Fire Support Base Maureen. A heavily armed force of enemy sappers and infantrymen assaulted Company D's night defensive position, wounding and killing a number of its members. Disregarding the intense enemy fire and ground assault, Pfc. Kays began moving toward the perimeter to assist his fallen comrades. In doing so he became the target of concentrated enemy fire and explosive charges, one of which severed the lower portion of his left leg. After applying a tourniquet to his leg, Pfc. Kays moved to the fire-swept perimeter, administered medical aid to one of the wounded, and helped move him to an area of relative safety. Despite his severe wound and excruciating pain, Pfc. Kays returned to the perimeter in search of other wounded men. He treated another wounded comrade, and, using his own body as a shield against enemy bullets and fragments, moved him to safety. Although weakened from a great loss of blood, Pfc. Kays resumed his heroic lifesaving efforts by moving beyond the company's perimeter into enemy held territory to treat a wounded American lying there. Only after his fellow wounded soldiers had been treated and evacuated did Pfc. Kays allow his own wounds to be treated. These courageous acts by Pfc. Kays resulted in the saving of numerous lives and inspired others in his company to repel the enemy. Pfc. Kays' heroism at the risk of his life are in keeping with the highest traditions of the service and reflect great credit on him, his unit, and the United States Army.

Appendix B

Distinguished Service Cross Citation for
Kenneth J. David

For extraordinary heroism in connection with military operations involving conflict with an armed hostile force in the Republic of Vietnam; Private First Class David distinguished himself while serving as radio-telephone operator during combat operations at an allied fire support base. During the early morning hours of 7 May 1970, Private David's company came under an intense attack from a large hostile force. Supported by intense small and automatic weapons fire, the enemy inflicted numerous casualties upon the allies and left Private David alone to defend his portion of the defensive perimeter. Unleashing a barrage of automatic weapons fire, the private bitterly resisted all enemy efforts to overrun his position. When the enemy began to toss satchel charges in the direction of the wounded allied soldiers, Private David began to shout in a manner which attracted the enemy's attention away from the allied casualties. Refusing to withdraw in the face of the concentrated fire now directed toward him, the private continued to resist the attackers in a determined manner. Although wounded by an exploding satchel charge and running perilously low on ammunition, he tossed hand grenades toward the attackers to effectively counter their fire. Then, after allied reinforcements fought their way to his position, Private David carried a wounded comrade to a sheltered position and returned to the contact area to engage the enemy until they broke contact and fled. Private First Class David's extraordinary heroism and devotion to duty were in keeping with the highest traditions of the military service and reflect great credit upon himself, his unit, and the United States Army.

Appendix C

Silver Star Citation for Gregory P. Phillips

For gallantry in action in the Republic of Vietnam on 7 May 1970. Specialist Phillips distinguished himself while serving as a grenadier in Company D 1st Battalion (Airmobile), 506th Infantry, defending Fire Support Base Maureen, Republic of Vietnam. While situated in night defensive positions, the company came under intense fire from a large, heavily armed enemy force, and there were numerous friendly casualties. Specialist Phillips, maneuvering to the hardest-hit sector of the perimeter, effectively engaged the hostiles with grenade fire. Depleting his ordnance, he obtained a rifle and, despite hostile fire, assaulted enemy positions outside the perimeter. When wounded, he maintained his heavy volume of suppressive fire. Finding a wounded comrade, he carried the man to safety. Specialist Phillips' personal bravery and devotion to duty were in keeping with the highest traditions of the military service and reflect great credit upon himself, his unit, and the United States Army.

Appendix D

Bronze Star with "V" Device Citation for
Stephen G. Avgerinos

For heroism in ground combat against a hostile force in the Republic of Vietnam on 7 May 1970. Sergeant Avgerinos distinguished himself while serving as a platoon sergeant in Company D, 1st Battalion (Airmobile), 506th Infantry, during combat action on Fire Support Base Maureen, Republic of Vietnam. While Sergeant Avgerinos's unit was in night defensive positions, the southern portion of the base perimeter came under an intense enemy attack, and numerous friendly soldiers were wounded. Sergeant Avgerinos, obtaining a radio, directed the fire of his men and called for aerial rocket artillery support. Despite being subjected to the hostile barrage, he continued to adjust rocket fire, then maneuvered to aid wounded comrades. His actions kept the aggressors from overrunning the fire base and helped keep friendly casualties at a minimum. Sergeant Avgerinos's personal bravery and devotion to duty were in keeping with the highest traditions of the military service and reflect great credit upon himself, his unit, and the United States Army.

Notes

Introduction

1. Edward F. Murphy, *Korean War Heroes* (Novato, Calif.: Presidio Press: 1992), 1.

2. B. G. Burkett and Glenna Whitley, *Stolen Valor: How the Vietnam Generation Was Robbed of its Hero and its History* (Dallas, Tex.: Verity Press: 1998), 353.

3. Lewis Sorley, *A Better War: The Unexamined Victories and Final Tragedy of America's Last Year in Vietnam* (New York: Harcourt Brace & Co., 1999), 205.

4. Gary A. Linderer in Frank Johnson, *Diary of an Airborne Ranger* (New York: Ballantine Books, 2001).

5. John Smith, interview with the author.

6. *Wayne County Press*, 29 July 2002.

1. Down in Egypt

1. "President Diem to President Kennedy," in Marvin E. Gettlemen et al., eds., *Vietnam and America: The Most Comprehensive Documented History of the Vietnam War* (New York: Grove Press, 1995), 163.

2. Ibid.

3. In Andrew Carroll, *War Letters: Extraordinary Correspondence From American War* (New York: Washington Square Press, 2001), 392–393.

4. In Steven M. Gillon, *The American Paradox: A History of the United States Since 1960* (Boston: Houghton Mifflin Co., 2003), 35.

5. Thomas Powers, *The War at Home: Vietnam and the American People* (New York: Grossman, 1973), 31.

6. Melvin Small, *Antiwarriors: The Vietnam War and the Battle for America's Hearts and Minds* (Wilmington, Del.: SR Books, 2002), 18, 85.

7. Taylor Pensoneau, *Brothers Notorious: The Sheltons, Southern Illinois' Legendary Gangsters* (New Berlin, Ill.: Downstate Publications, 2002), 263.

8. *Wayne County Press*, 20 January 1969.

9. Ibid., 30 January 1969.

10. Ibid.

11. Ibid., 8 March 1971.

12. Ibid.

13. Ibid., 8 February 1971.

14. Ibid., 12 August 1964, 15 August 1964.

15. Ibid., 20 January 1969.

16. Ibid., 24 February 1969.

17. Ibid., 5 November 1964.

18. Ibid., 23 January 1969.

19. Ibid.

20. Ibid., 24 February 1969.

21. See Jon Musgrave, *Egyptian Tales of Southern Illinois* (Marion: Illinois History, 2000), for an elaboration of how the region came by its unusual name.

22. Richard Powell, *Planting Corn Belt Culture: The Impress of the Upland Southern and Yankee in the Old Northwest* (Indianapolis: Indiana Historical Society, 1953), 1.

23. Edwin Sparks, ed., *The Lincoln Douglas Debate of 1858*, Vol. I (Springfield: Illinois Historical Library, 1908), 249.

24. Rufus Babcock, ed., *Forty Years of Pioneer Life: Memoirs of John Mason Peck* (Philadelphia: American Baptist Publication Society, 1864), 37.

25. Morris Birkbeck, *Notes on a Journey to America* (London: Severn and Co., 1818), 119, 108.

26. Paul M. Angle, *Bloody Williamson: A Chapter in American Lawlessness* (Urbana: University of Illinois Press, 1992), 72–73, XVI.

27. Baker Brownell, *The Other Illinois* (New York: Duell, Sloan, and Pearce, 1958), 14.

28. Ibid., 92.

29. *Southern Illinoisan*, 9 December 1956.

30. Brownell, *The Other Illinois*, 92.

31. In Pensoneau, *Brothers Notorious*, vi.

32. Ibid., vi–vii.

33. *Wayne County Press*, 19 August 2002.

2. Where Have All the Flowers Gone?

1. Pensoneau, *Brothers Notorious*, 275.

2. *Wayne County Press*, 1 December 1949, 29 December 1949.

3. Ibid., 20 November 1969.

4. Ibid., 3 August 1964.

5. Ibid., 20 August 1964.

6. Ibid., 8 May 1967.

7. Ibid., 5 May 1967.

8. Ibid., 8 May 1967.

9. Ibid., 5 May 1967.

10. Todd Gitlin, *The Sixties: Years of Hope, Days of Rage* (New York: Bantam Books, 1993), 195.

11. *Wayne County Press*, 14 October 1964.

12. Ibid., 23 July 1964.

13. *Newsweek*, 30 October 1967.

14. Ibid., 20 November 1967.

15. Ibid., 13 November 1967.

16. Ibid., 13 November 1967.

17. *Wayne County Press*, 11 May 1967.

18. Ibid., 6 November 1964.

19. Ibid., 19 January 1964.

20. *Newsweek*, 24 April 1967.

21. *Wayne County Press*, 18 May 1967.

22. Ibid., 20 May 1967.

3. A Party School

1. Betty Mitchell, *Delyte Morris of SIU* (Carbondale: Southern Illinois University Press, 1988).

2. Ibid., 13.

3. Brownell, *The Other Illinois*, 235, 237.

4. Mitchell, *Delyte Morris of SIU*, 24.

5. *Time*, 1964.

6. *Newsweek*, 12 June 1967.

7. *Christian Science Monitor*, 17 July 1968.

8. *Daily Egyptian*, 16 October 1998.

9. Ibid., 31 October 1970.

10. Small, *Antiwarriors.*

11. Ibid., 86.

12. Brian K. Clurdy, *The Management of Dissent: Responses to the Post Kent State Protests at Seven Public Universities in Illinois* (Lanham, Md.: University Press of America, 2002), 48.

13. Robbie Lieberman and David Cochrum, "There's Something Happening Here: 1960s Student Protest of Southern Illinois University Carbondale," paper presented at the Fourteenth Annual Conference of the Mid-America American Studies Association, 24–25 April 1998, Iowa City, Iowa, 8. See also same authors, "We Closed Down the School: the Party Culture at Southern Illinois University During the Vietnam War Era," *Peace and Change* 16 (July 2001), 326.

14. *Newsweek*, 10 July 1967.

15. Mitchell, *Delyte Morris of SIU*, 162.

16. *Christian Science Monitor*, 17 July 1968.

17. *Southern Illinoisan*, 27 May 1969.

18. *Wayne County Press*, 3 November 1969.

19. Ibid., 11 May 1970.

20. Ibid., 14 May 1970.

21. Ibid., 13 May 1971.

22. Ibid., 21 May 1970.

23. Terry H. Anderson, *The Movement and the Sixties* (Boston: Oxford University Press, 1996).

24. *Wayne County Press*, 23 January 1969.

25. Ibid., 27 November 1969.

26. Ibid., 4 December 1969.

27. Ibid., 25 December 1969.

28. Ibid., 11 December 1969.

29. Ibid., 10 July 2003.

30. In Small, *Antiwarriors*, 123.

31. *Daily Egyptian*, 8 June 1969.
32. Ibid.
33. In Mitchell, *Delyte Morris of SIU*, 208.

4. I Felt I Was Born That Weekend

1. *Newsweek*, 23 July 1969.
2. Ibid., 14 April 1969, 21 April 1969.
3. Ibid., 2 June 1969.
4. Ibid.
5. Ibid., 9 June 1969.
6. Neil Sheehan, "Letters From Hamburger Hill," *Harper's Magazine*, November 1969.
7. In *Twentieth Century America*, Associated Press, 1995, 77.
8. *Newsweek*, 1 September 1969.
9. Anderson, *The Movement and the Sixties*, 314.
10. In Harry Maurer, *Strange Ground: An Oral History of America in Vietnam* (New York: Dacapo Press, 1998), 224.
11. These testimonials about Woodstock and the testimony of scores of others can be found at http://www.woodstock69.com/woodstock_mem2.htm.
12. Ibid.
13. Ibid.
14. *Newsweek*, 25 August 1969.
15. *Wayne County Press*, 21 August 1969.
16. Ibid., 1 September 1969
17. Ibid.
18. Ibid., 11 August 1969.
19. Ibid., 28 August 1969.
20. Ibid., 1 September 1969.
21. Ibid., 25 August 1969.
22. Ibid., 25 September 1969.
23. Ibid., 25 August 1969.

5. Maybe I Can Help Somebody

1. *Wayne County Press*, 25 September 1969.
2. In Associated Press, *Twentieth Century America*, 78.
3. *Newsweek*, 13 October 1969.
4. Ibid.
5. James W. Tollefson, *The Strength Not to Fight: Conscientious Objectors of the Vietnam War* (Washington, D.C.: Brassey's, 2000), 8.
6. *Wayne County Press*, 8 September 1969.
7. Small, *Antiwarriors*.
8. *Newsweek*, 6 October 1969.

9. In Small, *Antiwarriors*, 111.

10. Joseph C. Goulden, "Voices from the Silent Majority" *Harper's Magazine* (April 1970), 67.

11. *Wayne County Press*, 13 November 1969.

12. Tollefson, *The Strength Not to Fight*, 153.

13. Ibid., 143.

14. Ibid., 108.

6. My Life Changed Forever

1. For the impact of World War II on young men who fought in Korea, see Randy Mills and Roxanne Mills, *Unexpected Journey: A Marine Corps Reserve Company in the Korean War* (Annapolis, Md.: Naval Institute Press, 2002).

2. For a detailed examination of this portion of the war, see Sorley, *A Better War*.

7. They Stood Alone

1. *Harper's Magazine*, November 1969.

2. Keith Nolan, *Ripcord: Screaming Eagles Under Siege, Vietnam 1970* (Novato, Calif.: Presidio Press, 2000), 10.

3. *Wayne County Press*, 7 January 1971.

4. Copies of official reports can be found on the 506th Regiment's website: http://www.506infantry.org/body.htm.

5. Nolan, *Ripcord*, 93. Nolan's account incorrectly has Steve "Greek" Avgerinos and Ken David killed in the initial attack, and other accounts have followed suit. Both Greek and Ken David have requested I emphasize that the two former 101st troopers are still alive and kicking.

6. See for example Gary Linderer, "The 101st Airborne Division: The Vietnam Experiences" in Robert J. Martin, *101st Airborne Division Screaming Eagles* (Paducah, Ky.: Turner Publishing Co., 1995), 74. Linderer essentially tells the same story as Keith Nolan.

7. In Benjamin L. Harrison, *Hell on a Hilltop: America's Last Major Battle in Vietnam* (New York: iUniverse Inc., 2004), 51.

8. Distinguished Service Cross citation for Kenneth David.

9. Congressional Medal of Honor citation for Kenneth Kays. Oddly, after intensive research, I have been unable to find any survivors, other than Gib Rossetter, who remember seeing Kays' actions in the battle. The procedure for writing up a recommendation for a Medal of Honor requires several firsthand accounts, as evident by the narrative of Kays' citation. Apparently, those involved in the process are either dead now or I was unable to locate them. Some survivors of the battle chose not to be interviewed or could not be located. Captain Workman, the company's leader who would have played a major role in the recommendation, was killed soon after Maureen.

8. Just a Damn Piece of Metal

1. *Wayne County Press,* 11 May 1970.
2. Edward Murphy, *Vietnam Medal of Honor Heroes* (New York: Ballantine Books, 1987), 250.
3. *Wayne County Press,* 7 January 1971.
4. Murphy, *Vietnam Medal of Honor Heroes,* 250.
5. *Wayne County Press,* 16 October 1973.
6. Ibid.
7. Ibid., 18 October 1973.
8. Murphy, *Vietnam Medal of Honor Heroes,* 250.
9. Ibid.
10. *Washington Post,* 16 October 1973.
11. *Wayne County Press,* 22 October 1973.
12. Ibid., 4 April 1974.
13. Ibid., 2 May 1974.
14. Ibid., 6 May 1974.
15. Ibid., 3 June 1974.
16. Ibid., 3 June 1971.
17. Ibid., 6 June 1974.
18. Ibid., 3 June 1974.
19. *Los Angeles Times,* 4 June 1974, 6 June 1974.
20. *Sedalia Democrat,* 13 June 1974.
21. *Wayne County Press,* 6 June 1974.
22. Ibid., 17 June 1974.
23. *St. Louis Post Dispatch,* 6 June 1974.
24. *Wayne County Press,* 3 June 1974.
25. Ibid., 7 January 1971.
26. Ibid., 2 May 1974.
27. Murphy, *Vietnam Medal of Honor Heroes,* 252.
28. *Wayne County Press,* 30 July 1979.
29. Ibid., 13 August 1979.
30. Ibid., 29 August 1979.
31. Ibid., 27 August 1979.
32. Ibid., 29 July 2002.
33. Ibid., 2 December 1991.
34. Ibid., 16 December 1991.
35. Ibid.
36. Ibid.
37. Ibid., 12 December 1991.

9. Back in the World

1. *Evansville Courier and Press,* 16 February 2002.
2. *Wayne County Press,* 29 July 2002.

3. Ibid., 19 August 2002.
4. Ibid., 29 August 2002.
5. Ibid., 10 July 2003.
6. *Evansville Courier and Press*, 16 February 2002.
7. *Wayne County Press*, 1 March 2004.
8. *Warren (Ohio) Tribune Chronicle*, 14 July 2003.

Note on Sources

Personal interviews, both oral and written, provided the bulk of the information used in this book. Complete copies of transcripts of these interviews are housed in the Oakland City University Barger-Richeson Library Archives. The following people shared their insights through interviews regarding Ken Kays' early years, his Southern Illinois University and Woodstock experiences, and his final days before he took his life: Kenny Boster, Rodney Cross, Douglas Gowler, Joe Keoughan, John Keoughan, Terry McGaha, Marshall Mills, Mike Pottorff, Randy Reed, Jon Simpson, Aaron Steiner, and David Trovillion (Steiner). Kays' experiences in Vietnam were made more understandable through the interviews of the following: John "Curt" Alexander, Steve "Greek" Avgerinos, Michael Bookser, Tony Cox, Kenneth David, Sammy L. Davis (Medal of Honor recipient), Richard "Dick" Doyle, Richard Drury, Dean Finch, Steve Gunn, Kurt Maag, Ralph Matkin, Larry McElroy, Greg Phillips, Gilbert "Gib" Rossetter, Gordon Scheerhorn, John Smith, and Dale Tauer. A number of personal letters were made available for this work by Michael Bookser, Kenneth David, and Steve Gunn. These letters greatly assisted the author in conveying a better understanding of the conditions faced by those who served in Vietnam. Portions of Kenneth Kays' personal journal were provided by Michael Pottorff. Several newspapers were used in this project, including the *Wayne County Press*, the *Evansville Courier*, the *Evansville Courier and Press*, the *Southern Illinoisan*, the Southern Illinois University student newspaper, the *Daily Egyptian*, the *Los Angeles Times*, the *St. Louis Post-Dispatch*, and the *Washington Post*. Microfilm copies of these newspapers can be found respectively in the following libraries: Fairfield Public Library, Fairfield, Illinois; Willard Library Special Collections, Evansville, Indiana; University of Southern Illinois Library, Carbondale, Illinois; and the Indiana University Main Library, Bloomington, Indiana.

Bibliography

Anderson, David L. ed., *Shadow on the White House: Presidents and the Vietnam War, 1945–1975*. Lawrence: University Press of Kansas, 1993.

Anderson, Terry H. *The Movement and the Sixties*. Boston: Oxford University Press, 1996.

Angle, Paul M. *Bloody Williamson: A Chapter in American Lawlessness*. Urbana: University of Illinois Press, 1992.

Babcock, Rufus, ed. *Forty Years of Pioneer Life: Memoirs of John Mason Peck*. Philadelphia: American Baptist Publication Society, 1864.

Birkbeck, Morris. *Notes on a Journey to America*. London: Severn and Co., 1818.

Brownell, Baker. *The Other Illinois*. New York: Duell, Sloan, and Pearce, 1958.

Burkett, B. G., and Glenna Whitley. *Stolen Valor: How the Vietnam Generation Was Robbed of its Hero and its History*. Dallas, Tex.: Verity Press, 1998.

Carroll, Andrew. *War Letters: Extraordinary Correspondence From American War*. New York: Washington Square Press, 2001.

Clurdy, Brian K. *The Management of Dissent: Responses to the Post Kent State Protests at Seven Public Universities in Illinois*. Lanham, Md.: University Press of America, 2002.

Edelman, Bernard. *Dear America: Letters Home from Vietnam*. New York: W. W. Norton & Co., 1985.

Gettlemen, Marvin E., et al., eds. *Vietnam and America: The Most Comprehensive Documented History of the Vietnam War*. New York: Grove Press, 1995.

Gillon, Steven M. *The American Paradox: A History of the United States Since 1960*. Boston: Houghton Mifflin Co., 2003.

Gitlin, Todd. *The Sixties: Years of Hope, Days of Rage*. New York: Bantam Books, 1993.

Harrison, Benjamin L. *Hell on a Hilltop: America's Last Major Battle in Vietnam*. New York: iUniverse, Inc., 2004.

Lieberman, Robbie, and David Cochrum, "There's Something Happening Here: 1960s Student Protest of Southern Illinois University Carbondale." Paper presented at the Fourteenth Annual Conference of the Mid-America American Studies Association, 24–25 April 1998, Iowa City, Iowa.

———. "We Closed Down the School: the Party Culture at Southern Illinois University During the Vietnam War Era," *Peace and Change* 16 (July 2001).

Linderer, Gary A., in Frank Johnson. *Diary of an Airborne Ranger*. New York: Ballantine Books, 2001.

———. "The 101st Airborne Division: The Vietnam Experiences," in Robert J. Martin, ed., *101st Airborne Division Screaming Eagles*. Paducah, Ky.: Turner Publishing Co., 1995.

Maurer, Harry. *Strange Ground: An Oral History of America in Vietnam*. New York: Dacapo Press, 1998.

Mills, Randy, and Roxanne Mills. *Unexpected Journey: A Marine Corps Reserve Company in the Korean War*. Annapolis, Md.: Naval Institute Press, 2002.

Milton, Bates, ed. *Reporting Vietnam: American Journalism 1954–1975*. New York: The Library of America, 2000.

Mitchell, Betty. *Delyte Morris of SIU*. Carbondale: Southern Illinois University Press, 1988.

Murphy, Edward F. *Korean War Heroes*. Novato, Calif.: Presidio Press, 1992.

———. *Vietnam Medal of Honor Heroes*. New York: Ballantine Books, 1987.

Musgrave, Jon. *Egyptian Tales of Southern Illinois*. Marion: Illinois History, 2000.

Nolan, Keith. *Ripcord: Screaming Eagles Under Siege, Vietnam 1970*. Novato, Calif.: Presidio Press, 2000.

Pensoneau, Taylor. *Brothers Notorious: the Sheltons, Southern Illinois' Legendary Gangsters*. New Berlin, Ill.: Downstate Publications, 2002.

Powell, Richard. *Planting Corn Belt Culture: The Impress of the Upland Southern and Yankee in the Old Northwest*. Indianapolis: Indiana Historical Society, 1953.

Powers, Thomas. *The War at Home: Vietnam and the American People*. New York: Grossman, 1973.

Santoli, Al. *Everything We Had: An Oral History of the Vietnam War by Thirty-Three American Soldiers Who Fought It*. New York: Putnam House, 1981.

Shay, Jonathan. *Achilles in Vietnam*. New York: Simon and Schuster, 1994.

Small, Melvin. *Antiwarriors: the Vietnam War and the Battle for America's Hearts and Minds*. Wilmington, Del.: SR Books, 2002.

Sorley, Lewis. *A Better War: The Unexamined Victories and Final Tragedy of America's Last Year in Vietnam*. New York: Harcourt Brace & Co., 1999.

Sparks, Edwin, ed., *The Lincoln Douglas Debate of 1858*, Vol. I. Springfield: Illinois Historical Library, 1908.

Tollefson, James W. *The Strength Not to Fight: Conscientious Objectors of the Vietnam War*. Washington, D.C.: Brassey's, 2000.

Tucker, Spencer C., ed., *The Encyclopedia of the Vietnam War: A Political, Social, and Military History*. New York: Oxford University Press, 1998.

Zaffiri, Samuel. *Hamburger Hill*. Novato, Calif.: Presidio Press, 1998.

Index

Page numbers in italics refer to illustrations.

RANDY K. MILLS is Professor of the Social Sciences at Oakland City University and author of *Unexpected Journey: A Marine Corps Reserve Company in the Korean War* (with Roxanne Mills); *Those Who Paid the Price: Forgotten Voices from the Korean War*; and *Jonathan Jennings: Indiana's First Governor*.